KV-513-065

TELEPEN

1575452904

LOOKING INTO WORLD RELIGIONS

BEING A MUSLIM

ANGELA WOOD

B.T. BATSFORD LTD   LONDON

CONTENTS

For Maqbul Ahmed Siddiqui, who first showed me what being a Muslim really means

Frontispiece:
"Seek knowledge even though it is in China". With these words, recorded in the hadith, the Prophet Muhammad conveyed to Muslims that there are no lengths to which you should not go to get an education and that it is not enough to be learned; we have to go on learning all our lives. Many young Muslims, like these in Britain, go to a State school all week and then attend classes at the mosque at weekends or after school. There they meet other Muslims of the same age, learn Arabic, read and discuss the Qur'an, and explore the world of Muslim culture. These girls express different attitudes and backgrounds in their dress but their approach to Qur'anic study is identical: concentration and respect.

ACKNOWLEDGMENTS
The Author and Publishers would like to thank the following for permission to reproduce copyright illustrations: Associated Press, page 53; Camerapix Magazines Ltd, pages 7, 29, 41 and 47; Sally and Richard Greenhill, frontispiece; Hutchinson Library, front cover colour (John Egan) and pages 10, 15 (Jill Brown), 44 and 50 (John Egan); Anne and Bury Peerless, page 22; Photosource, pages 17, 20 (and front cover), 26, 33, 38, 54 and 58 (and front cover); Karena J. Smith, page 13.

The Author would like to give her special thanks to Sheikh Solaiman. Also to Karena J. Smith, who researched the pictures.

First published 1987

Typeset by Tek-Art Ltd, West Wickham, Kent
Printed in Great Britain by
R J Acford Ltd,
Chichester, Sussex
for the publishers
B.T. Batsford Ltd,
4 Fitzhardinge Street, London W1H 0AH

ISBN 0 7134 4667 6

INTRODUCTION

More than one in seven of the world's population is Muslim, and it is the fastest growing religious tradition in the world today. It took formal shape some 1400 years ago in Saudi Arabia, but Muslims themselves say that it is for all people at all times and in all places. They also stress that Islam began when the universe began and that the first prophet was the first human being – Adam.

More than a religion in a purely spiritual sense, Islam is a system of government and law, and a way of life under God. The impulse to spread Islam has existed from the time of the Prophet Muhammad, and much effort has been made to convert polytheists (those who believe in more than one god) and atheists (those who don't believe in any god). But Muslims have always had a different attitude to Jews and Christians, whom they see as monotheists (those who believe in one God) like them, standing in the same tradition, sharing many values and paving the way for the final revelation. While intermarriage generally is forbidden in Islam, a Muslim *man* is allowed to marry a Jew or a Christian. That is merely one sign of the special relationship between them.

This book looks at what being a Muslim means and emphasizes the activities and experiences that are part of being Muslim, for being *is* doing. That is why the title of each section includes an "____ing" word. The book begins by looking at definite *actions* that are quite easy to understand, then moves through *emotions* of loving, losing and belonging, to *spiritual sensations* of hoping, longing, believing and praying.

The idea that God used an angel to say to an illiterate man, "Recite!" places great emphasis on the spoken and written word, and that is why looking at Muslim sources is a good way to know what Islam, and Muslims, are like.

MUSLIM SOURCES

The quotations in this book come from several Muslim sources: most Muslims are agreed on what they should believe and how they should behave, but even so Muslims express these beliefs and ideas in different ways. In each section of the book, you will find quotations from three different kinds of written sources (although many were originally spoken, not written).

* First and foremost is the Qur'an, the most

ancient, authoritative Muslim text, the source of every other source.

* The second kind of source is *either* a *hadith* – one of the traditions of the Prophet Muhammad – which began to be recorded during his lifetime, about 1400 years ago; *or* a poem or parable from the vast mystical literature which spanned several centuries and which illuminates many Muslim ideas and values even if the form it takes is a little surprising.

* Thirdly, you will find quotations from sources of our own times. This might be an extract from a letter, diary, magazine article or "problem page", a television discussion, a snatch of conversation, a random thought, a community circular or newsletter, a sermon, a child's poem.

THE QUR'AN

For Muslims, the Qur'an is not only the "sacred book" and the source of law, but also a complete package from Allah intended for the whole human race. Muslims believe that Muhammad did not invent or create the Qur'an but that it was revealed to him by Jibrail (the angel Gabriel) over a period of 23 years – from when Muhammad was 40 until just before his death, that is, between 610 and 632 CE. The Qur'an *already* existed and the Qur'an you can buy in a bookshop is a perfect copy of that pre-existent scripture. That is why Muslims place such emphasis on exact memorization of the Qur'an.

The Prophet said that whenever Jibrail communicated new verses of the Qur'an he would made him repeat them as many times as was needed for him to know them by heart. Jibrail also told Muhammad the exact place to put the new verses in the growing collection of chapters and verses. The Qur'an is therefore not arranged in the same order in which it was revealed – but the arrangement was itself revealed!

The Prophet could not read or write: whenever something was revealed to him, he dictated it to one of his Companions, who would write it down and read it straight back to him for checking.

Many Arabs were illiterate, like the Prophet, but they had a long tradition of memorizing and preserving literature, so as soon as the Qur'an was revealed there were those who began to learn it by heart – and to recite it by heart – with love and devotion. During Muhammad's lifetime, there were five *huffaz* (people who had memorized the entire Qur'an).

The Qur'an was originally written on several different kinds of material – parchment, leaves, bones, pieces of leather – so when the Prophet died Abu Bakr (the first *khalifa*, or successor) asked Zaid ibn Thabit, who had been Muhammad's chief scribe of revelations, to collect the entire Qur'an together. It was then written out in a single volume, supervised by a committee. The language used was the Mudar dialect, spoken by the Quraish clan (to which the Prophet had belonged), as this was the language in which the Qur'an had been revealed. Then the five *huffaz*, along with other Companions, looked carefully at the final version and they agreed it was accurate and authentic. Within two years of the Prophet's death this was completed: the perfect copy was given to Aisha, the Prophet's widow and the daughter of Abu Bakr.

Umar, the second *khalifa*, started many schools for teaching the Qur'an but the third *khalifa*, Uthman, found out that in some places where people did not speak Arabic there were some new Muslims who were not pronouncing the Qur'an correctly. He arranged to have all their copies of the Qur'an recalled and replaced by copies of the standard version (which was with Aisha). That was 651 CE, and the Qur'an printed today is absolutely identical. Muslims say that Allah protects the Qur'an from having anything added, removed or changed in any way and the Qur'an says about itself that Allah has sent down the message and will guard it from corruption (15:9).

The Qur'an is divided into 114 *surahs* (chapters), 86 of which were revealed in Makka and 28 in Madina. The number of *ayahs* (verses) varies from *surah* to *surah*: Surah 2 is the longest with 286 *ayahs*, while Surahs 103, 108 and 110 only have three *ayahs* each. A given *surah* may contain revelations on various dates, covering different subjects. Some verses from Madina are in a *surah* called "Makka". Some of the Madina *surahs* which were revealed later come first in the Qur'an and some early Makkan *surahs* appear near the end.

Strictly speaking, the Qur'an cannot be translated, both because much of its subtlety and inner meaning is lost in translation and simply because it was *revealed* in Arabic! But most Muslims today are not Arabic speakers and although they use the original for their devotions they need a translation in their own language for information and discussion. When the Qur'an is used in another language it is usually called an "interpretation", or "the meaning of the Qur'an", suggesting that it is not altogether reliable or genuine.

In this book, quotations from the Qur'an are selected from one of the most modern versions in English undertaken by Muslim scholars: *The Qur'an: Basic Teachings*, by Thomas Ballantine Irving, Khurshid Ahmad and Muhammad Manazir Ahsan, published by The Islamic Foundation in 1979.

HADITH

Throughout the Prophet's lifetime Muslims realized they could learn not only from what had been revealed to Muhammad but also from his own behaviour.

Sunnah is Arabic for "practice" and refers to whatever the Prophet did as the Messenger of Allah which should be followed by Muslims. For example, how the Prophet performed washing before prayer is *sunnah* but how he drank water is not!

A *hadith* is a verbal report or tradition, originally transmitted by word of mouth, of what the Prophet said or did. There are perhaps examples of *sunnah* without *hadith* and there are many *ahadith* (plural) without any reported *sunnah*.

Companions of the Prophet would report to others what they had seen him do or heard him say and that was passed on to others to form a chain called *isnad*. When *ahadith* were compiled, the *isnad* of each one was stated so that it could be traced back to the Prophet. The two most reliable books of *hadith* are the *Sahih of Bukhari* and the *Sahih of Muslim*. With four other works, they form the "accurate six", all compiled in the third century of the Islamic era.

Ahadith have been divided into three main groups: *sahih* (sound); *hasan* (good); and *da'if*, or *saqim* (weak).

Early on, the *muhadithin* (collectors of *ahadith*) developed criteria for assessing whether a *hadith* was authentic: the *isnad* had to stretch back to a specific person who was actually present when the story being told took place; each person in the *isnad* had to be reliable; and the *hadith* itself had to be believable. A *hadith* was thought to be *unbelievable* if it went against the Qur'an, *sunnah* or sound *hadiths*; if it made the Prophet look or sound a fool; if it contradicted well-known evidence or observable facts; if it reported an event which should have been witnessed by hundreds of people but had, in fact, been reported by only one; if it used rude words; if it prophesied events, giving definite dates; if it threatened great punishments for small mistakes or promised great rewards for small good deeds.

BEING A MUSLIM

"Assalamu aleikum! ("Peace be upon you!") is the Arabic greeting Muslims use all over the world, whatever language they speak, when they meet and when they part. The reply "Wa aleikum salam!" ("Upon *you* peace!") reinforces peace – that complete harmony between people and within a person – as the ideal at the heart of Islam. What this really involves is surrendering yourself to Allah unconditionally, and Muslims express this in ritual actions and in acts of loving kindness; for Muslims, surrendering to Allah does not mean denying themselves but actually finding their true selves, both accepting themselves and trying to improve themselves.

Some Muslim scholars have said that to be a Muslim is to act totally in accordance with one's

"Labbaika!" ("Here I am!") Muslims call out on their way to Makka and as they reach the Ka'ba the excitement grows, the commitment intensifies and the surrender to Allah is complete. Going on pilgrimage to Makka is a once-in-a-lifetime experience, but being a Muslim is an experience that lasts throughout your life.

nature. When asked whether a dog could be a Muslim they answered: yes, because a dog is always "doggy": a dog is not a good dog or a bad dog or only sometimes a dog – a dog is a dog. It's only humans who are good or bad – who sometimes "play God", who try to be superhuman but often act in a subhuman way. So it is only *people* who can be non-Muslim! Islam is the fulfilment of their humanity.

BEING AND HAVING

Being a Muslim does not depend on what you have but on what you believe – that is, what you have inside you. So much depends on your attitude of mind and the choices you make for yourself. Usually it is hard to tell how much a person is shaped by what he or she has been given in life and how much by his or her own efforts of will.

Set forth the example of two men for them: We granted two vineyards to one of them, and bordered them with datepalms and planted field crops in between. Each garden produced its food and did not fail to yield its best; We even caused a river to spring forth in the midst of them.
One man had fruit [in abundance] and told his

companion while he was discussing things with him: "I am wealthier than you are, and have a bigger following." He entered his garden while he was thus harming his own soul. He said: "I think that this will never disappear. I do not think the [final] Hour is at hand. If I am ever sent back to my Lord, I shall find something better than it in exchange."

His companion told him while he was discussing things with him: "Have you disbelieved in the One Who created you from dust, then from a drop of semen; then fashioned you into a man? As for me, He is God my Lord, and I do not associate anyone with my Lord. Why, as you entered your garden, did you not say: 'Whatever God wills; there is no strength except through God [Alone]!?' Even if you see that I am less wealthy than you are and have

fewer children, perhaps my Lord will still give me something better than your garden and send a reckoning down from Heaven on it, so that it will become a bald hilltop, or its water will sink down and you will never manage to find it [again]."

His produce was destroyed and he began to wring his hands over what he had spent on it, since it had tumbled down from its trellises. He kept saying: "It is too bad for me; I should never have associated anyone with my Lord!"

He had no party to support him against God, so he was not supported. In such a situation [it becomes evident] that protection comes from the True God [Alone]. He is Best as a recompense and Best in results.

(Qur'an 18: 32-34)

STREAKY SAND

A folk tale expresses the need to be strong in one's identity and not someone who can be too easily changed:

There was once a woman who abandoned the religion in which she had been brought up. She left the ranks of the atheists, too, and joined another faith. Then she became convinced of the truth of yet another.

Each time she changed her beliefs, she imagined that she had gained something, but not quite enough. Each time she entered a new fold, she was welcomed, and her recruitment was regarded as a good thing and a sign of her sanity and enlightenment.

Her inward state, however, was one of confusion. At length she heard of a certain celebrated teacher, and she went to see him. After he had listened to her protestations and ideas, he said, 'Return to your home. I shall send you my decision in a message.'

Soon afterwards the woman found a disciple of the sheikh at the door. In his hand was a packet from his master. She opened it, and saw that it contained a glass bottle, half-full with three layers of packed sand — black, red and white — held down by a wad of cotton. On the outside was written: 'Remove the cotton and shake the bottle to see what you are like.'

She took the wadding out, and shook the sand in the bottle. The different coloured grains of sand mixed together, and all that she was left with was — a mass of greyish sand.

(Idries Shah, "Streaky Sand", *Thinkers of the East*, Penguin, 1971, p. 77)

BLACK AND WHITE

The idea that Islam is a religion and a total way of life open to people of all races, has been from the days of the Prophet: Muhammad's last sermon touched on the theme of human equality. But there are many things in life that we *know* to be true which take a certain experience for us to feel to be true. Al Hajj Malik al-Shabazz — born as Malcolm Little — is better known to the public as Malcolm X, the Black American Muslim radical who died in 1965 at the hands of an assassin. The previous year, when in Makka, he kept a diary and in it he wrote of the insight he gained there of what it means to be a Muslim.

During the past eleven days here in the Muslim world, I have eaten from the same plate, drunk from the same glass, and slept in the same bed (or on the same rug) — while praying to the *same God* — with fellow Muslims, whose eyes were the bluest of blue, whose hair was the blondest of blond, and whose skin was the whitest of white. And in the *words* and in the *actions* and in the *deeds* of the 'white' Muslims, I felt the same sincerity that I felt among the black African Muslims of Nigeria, Sudan and Ghana.

We were truly all the same (brothers) — because their belief in one God had removed the 'white' from their *minds*, the 'white' from their *behavior*, and the 'white' from their *attitude*.

(*The Autobiography of Malcolm X*, Penguin, 1985, pp. 454-5)

BEING MARRIED

Islamic law has more to say about Muslim marriage than about any other subject. There's a lot about roles and rights and responsibilities but, naturally, it is the relationship itself that makes or breaks a marriage. If you look at Muslim life across the world, you can see a wide range of lifestyles.

In some Muslim societies women don't go out to work: they concern themselves with child-bearing and child-rearing. They don't do any religious study, may not have been taught any of the Qur'an and may be illiterate. They have not been encouraged to think for themselves, so they may run the home on a day-to-day basis but play a very small part in the decision-making processes of the family and may have to accept choices made for them by their fathers, husbands or, occasionally, other males. Such a picture of Muslim family life is common in Western media and, while it's a true reflection of some parts of the Islamic world, the reality in other places is totally different.

In many Muslim societies today, women work outside the home and may have interesting and productive careers as doctors, teachers, television personalities, business personnel, computer programmers, and so on. They dress modestly but attractively, and their heads and faces are not covered up. Although they don't have sexual contact outside marriage they may mix freely with men at work, at social gatherings and in public. In a society like this, girls may be encouraged as much as boys to continue with their education and when they are married they expect to talk things over with their husband and to make important decisions together.

Between these two extremes range many patterns of Muslim family life and this is a clear example of the difference between local custom and Islam as a universal religion.

FOR HIS, OR HER, EYES ONLY!

Muslims feel that sexual love is for married people only, and for them to be faithful to each other they must not tempt other people or be tempted by them. That is why both men and women dress – and, more importantly, *act* – modestly.

Tell believers to avert their glances and to guard their private parts; that is purer for them. God is Informed about anything they may do. Tell believing women to avert their glances and guard their private parts, and not to display their charms except what [normally] appears of them. They should fold their shawls over their bosoms and show their charms only to their husbands, or their fathers or their fathers-in-law, or their own sons or stepsons, or their own brothers and nephews on either their brothers' or their sisters' side; or their own womenfolk, or anyone their right hands control [e.g. servants], or male attendants who have no sexual desire, or children who have not yet shown any interest in women's nakedness. Let them not stomp their feet in order to let any ornaments they may have hidden be noticed. Turn to God, all you believers, so that you may prosper.
(Qur'an 24: 30-31)

TWO BODIES BUT ONE SOUL

Jalalu'l-Din Rumi was a mystical poet who lived in Persia in the thirteenth century CE. He sees a relationship that is so close that the two become one. As the unity gets stronger and the harmony gets deeper, the lover and the beloved become love itself. Ordinary life disappears and they are transported to another world where the impossible happens: they can be in two places at once.

> HAPPY the moment when we are seated in the palace, thou and I,
> With two forms and with two figures but with one soul, thou and I.
> The colours of the grove and the voices of the birds will bestow immortality
> At the time when we shall come into the garden, thou and I.
> The stars of Heaven will come to gaze upon us:
> We shall show them the moon herself, thou and I.
> Thou and I, individuals no more, shall be mingled in ecstasy,
> Joyful and secure from foolish babble, thou and I.
> All the bright-plumed birds of Heaven will devour their hearts with envy
> In the place where we shall laugh in such a fashion, thou and I.
> This is the greatest wonder, that thou and I, sitting here in the same nook,
> Are at this moment both in 'Iraq and Khorasan, thou and I.

(Diwan, XXXVIII in R.A. Nicholson, *Rumi: Poet and Mystic*, George Allen and Unwin Ltd, 1978, p. 35)

WORKING IT OUT

Nawal el Sa'adawi is an Egyptian Muslim doctor and writer. She has campaigned for women's rights in Arab countries for many years. In an interview for a women's magazine in Britain she spoke about her mother and father and the way they brought her up; her husband and the need for cooperation and equality in a partnership marriage; and the ways she sees her own children becoming independent.

I have inherited a lot from my mother. Although my father respected her highly and she had lots of rights, she challenged him a lot. I remember her always saying that she especially resented being brought out of school to marry him. . . .

My parents encouraged independence in me. I do the same with my children from whom I also learn a lot. My husband and I are both very strong personalities, but we try to avoid imposing ourselves on our children. We do not expect them to obey us; in fact we allow them to challenge us. Their problems are different from ours, and they have to respond to them in their own way. That is how they have developed their personality. . . .

I do not have a servant; I cannot afford it. My husband and I share the house work, and we both enjoy helping each other out. I organise my day to fit in cooking and washing alongside my writing, seeing some patients and working with the local women in organising ourselves.

(Interview with Tsehai, "Nawal–Practising Feminism", *Spare Rib*, No. 169, August 1986, pp. 14-17)

For the Muslim woman, marriage and motherhood are inseparable, and the honour of the home is handed down from mother to daughter.

LOVING YOUR CHILDREN

Loving your children doesn't mean liking everything your children do or letting them go wild! Generally, Muslim parents are quite strict with their children, believing that it's in the young people's interests to learn to be good and to accept discipline from an early age. They hope that the children will eventually become self-disciplined and independent. However, in a few Muslim societies children are expected to be obedient to their parents, especially their fathers, all their lives – that is, until they themselves become the senior members of the family with all the power and responsibility that involves.

Some Muslim couples practise birth control to limit the size of their family or to "spread" the children out, and occasionally a Muslim does not

Piggy-back on your mother, whether in the Turkish mountains or elsewhere, is not always just for fun but also a way of life: it creates a deep bond between you and her and gives you a very special view of the world.

want to have children at all, but other Muslims find this very strange. Most Muslim families have several children and they are to them a blessing from Allah.

ZACHARIAH'S CRY

Muslims not only seem to love the children they have but also love to have children! One of the prophets of Islam is John. He was born just before Jesus, who, according to the Qur'an, is also a prophet. For a long time before he was born, John's parents thought they could not have children and Zachariah prayed for God to give him a child.

With that Zachariah appealed to his Lord; he said: "My Lord, grant me goodly offspring from Your Bounty, for You are the Hearer of appeal."
(Qur'an 3: 38)

THE SON OF A CAMEL

The Prophet Muhammad took life very seriously but also liked to tell and hear jokes. He sometimes used humour to help people understand a situation better. In this story he wanted to get across the idea that no one ever stops being a child.

A man went to Mohammed and asked him for a camel.

'I will give you the child of a camel,' said the Prophet.

'How can the child of a camel bear the weight of a huge man such as me?' asked the man.

'Quite easily,' said the Prophet; 'I will grant your wish and mine. Have this fully-grown camel – is it not the son of a camel?
(Idries Shah, *Caravan of Dreams*, Quartet Books, 1973, p. 13)

ALLAH'S CHILDREN

A Muslim mother argues that Islam does not have to be as stern as it sometimes appears; too many rules squash the children's natural spirit and stop them enjoying God's world.

A short time ago, a little girl I know approached me and asked whether music was 'haram' (forbidden) in Islam. She had been told that this was the case by her teachers at the class which she and other Muslim children attended every weekend in their home-town. She was obviously confused and upset by the bombardment of 'harams' she had received at these classes, particularly pertaining to what, for her and many others, is a source of innocent pleasure.

When I was a child I was taught that all nature glorifies God and submits to His will . . . God loves all that is beautiful: we need but look around at his creation to understand this. The natural world around us is alive with colour, activity, strange and wonderful forms, sounds sweet and powerful. The austerity our teachers preach jars with God's own creation.

. . .

It is time that Muslims and non-Muslims alike recognised the true essence of Islam. We must no longer frighten our children and quell their energy and enthusiasm with a huge burden of rules and regulations which have little or no real authority according to the only valid criterion for judgement: the Qur'an.

(Samira Sharif, "If Music be the food of love . . .", *Arabia: The Islamic World Review*, Vol. 5, No. 61, September 1986)

LOVING YOUR PARENTS

The Prophet Muhammad never really knew family life as a child: his father died before he was born and his mother when he was only six. For the next two years his grandfather looked after him, but when he died the young boy went to live with his uncle. So he had a very unstable childhood and, at an early age, had to mourn the death of several people who were close to him.

Perhaps it is surprising – or perhaps it is quite understandable – that he himself enjoyed married life and fatherhood as much as he did and attached such importance to the Muslim family: for its comfort and its control, for the

Wanting to be with Daddy and to work like Daddy is a natural response in a child. Islam encourages responses like that and tries to build firm family feelings. We can receive knowledge and skill from our parents as well as love, and it is by being close to our parents that we become apprentices in life.

insight it gives into the meaning of Islam, and for the inspiration it offers to lead a good life.

Muhammad did not invent this view of the family: he was himself inspired by the Qur'an, which was revealed to him. More of it is devoted to marriage and the family than to anything else.

NEVER SAY "OUGH!"

Kindness and respect for parents is not just for Muslim children and teenagers but lasts a lifetime – that is, it should go on until they die. Muslims believe they never stop being their parents' children, even when they have children of their own.

> Your Lord has decreed that you should worship nothing except Him, and [show] kindness to your parents; whether either or both of them attain old age [while they are] still with you, never say to them "Ough!" nor scold either of them. Speak to them in a generous fashion. Serve them with tenderness and humility, and SAY: "My Lord, show them mercy, just as they cared for me as a little child."
>
> (Qur'an 17: 23-5)

"MUM'S THE WORD"

A well-known and well-loved *hadith* expresses the honour due to your mother:

> **Abu Hurairah reported that a man asked the Messenger of Allah (peace and blessings of Allah be upon him) as to who amongst his near ones has the greatest right over him. He (the Holy Prophet) replied: 'Your mother.' He asked, 'Then who is (next)?' He (the Holy Prophet) replied: 'Your mother.' He again asked, 'Then who (is next)?' He (the Holy Prophet) replied: 'Your mother!' He asked: 'Then who is (next)?' He (the Holy Prophet) replied: 'Your father!'**
>
> (Abdul Hamid Siddique, *Selection from Hadith*, 127, Islamic Book Publishers, 1979, p. 69)

GROWING UP AS MUSLIMS

A young Muslim talks about the problems of *jahiliyah*, which is partly ignorance and partly laziness or lack of care for Islamic values. The pressure to assimilate is very strong indeed in a non-Muslim society but the Muslim family can protect and strengthen its members.

An ideal Islamic home is a home in which every member of the family knows the Islamic values and tries to practise them in the best way. These homes have blessings from Allah and are very peaceful, so when a Muslim kid walks in from a day at school, he or she feels comfortable and peaceful. The members of the family can understand the frustrations of the young Muslim when he or she gets exposed to annoying questions like "Why don't Muslims date?" or "Don't you get hot in that thing [scarf]?" What makes them annoying is that they ask the same questions every day. A good practising Muslim family can be real good support to a young growing Muslim or Muslimah in this day and age. The next thing that helps us deal with the jahiliyah is patience, lots of patience.

As a young Muslim or Muslimah, we need strong support from our community and family to deal with the jahiliyah. We are trying very hard and striving to become good practising Muslims.

(Usma Unus, "Growing up as Muslims in this day and age", *The Straight Path*, Vol. 7, No. 4, May 1986, pp. 26-7)

GETTING MARRIED

When two Muslims marry they fulfil Islamic law by signing a contract which confirms that they have exchanged marriage vows. There is no ceremony as such, though Muslim societies have developed lively customs to celebrate the occasion.

The wedding can take place anywhere, though in Muslim societies it is usually in a home and in Britain it is usually in a mosque. Islam has no priests and no one *needs* to perform the wedding: the two families could simply gather to exchange the agreement. But in practice the *imam* (leader of the mosque) is usually present, and he will often recite some relevant verses from the Qur'an, or retell a *hadith*, or simply speak informally about marriage. He may also help with the preparation of the *aqd nikah* (marriage contract).

One thing the husband has to do is make his

For most people, getting married is the most important step they ever take and their wedding day will be the most memorable of their life: it's no wonder they are nervous and shy! Some Muslim wedding customs in the Indian sub-continent are similar to Hindu or Sikh ways and quite different from practices in other parts of the Muslim world, such as Africa or the Middle East. For this wedding in Pakistan, the whole community has turned out, and it has the flavour of a festival. The couple are treated like royalty: they wear silk and jewels and are bedecked with garlands of tinsel and flowers.

wife a present, called *mahr*, over a period of time. It becomes her property and her husband can never claim it back. The Prophet Muhammad once answered a man who was worried that he could not afford *mahr* for his wife because he was so poor: "Give the best you have: teach her the Qur'an!"

MARRYING FOR LOVE AND MARRYING FOR FAITH

For Muslims, marriage is such an important relationship that they feel it cannot be based just on personal attraction between the man and the woman. Ideally, a Muslim should marry another Muslim, but at least he or she should not marry an associator – someone who "associates" something or someone with God. (People who worship idols are thought of as associators.) Sometimes Muslim men marry Jewish or Christian women (but Muslim women should only marry Muslim men).

Do not marry women who associate [others with God] until they believe. A believing maid is better than an associating woman, no matter how attractive she may seem to you.

Do not [let your women] marry men who associate [others with God] until the latter believe; a believing slave is better than an associator, no matter how attractive he may seem to you.

Those people invite [one] to the Fire while God invites [us] to the Garden and to forgiveness by His permission. He explains His signs to mankind so that they may bear them in mind.
(Qur'an 2: 221)

A SPECIAL ARRANGEMENT

Many Muslims look up to Muhammad and his wife, Khadija, as the ideal married couple. It is obvious that the conventions of marriage are not important because Khadija was 40 years old and Muhammad was only 25, Khadija was a business-woman and Muhammad was her employee, and Khadija was the one to propose marriage to Muhammad!

One day a surprising thing happened. Khadija's personal maid came to see Muhammad privately. She came with a marriage proposal from Khadija! Muhammad was astounded. He had never even had a girl-friend. He had never thought much about women, nor had he ever been close to one since the death of his mother. Some time back, when he was tending sheep, some shepherds passing by had called to him:

'Come to town with us tonight, Muhammad — we'll have a little fun with the girls!'

Muhammad, who liked the idea well enough, agreed to join them later. But he never turned up at the rendezvous. The following day the shepherds asked him:

'What happened to you last night?'

'Well', Muhammad confessed, 'when the time

came, I fell asleep'. Of course they all burst out laughing and he joined in with them.

But Khadija, in the eyes of Muhammad, was a very special lady. She was warm and kind, and still quite beautiful despite the fact that she was older than he. This time, Muhammad did not take long to accept. The marriage between Muhammad and Khadija took place, and turned out to be a very happy one.

(Mardijah Aldrich Tarantino, *Marvellous Stories from the Life of Muhammad*, The Islamic Foundation, 1982, pp. 29-30)

GIVE AND TAKE

Six young Muslim women studying in the Sixth Form of a British school discuss their views on marriage and what they are hoping for. Some of them see an important difference between Islam and the culture of the country they or their family come from – Pakistan. All of them are conscious, committed Muslims who want a true Islamic life in the modern world.

A lot of people ask me, "Are you going to have an arranged marriage?" And their idea is my mother and father pushing me into something I don't want to do, and those ideas are very frustrating because they don't realise that things are changing. . .

In our family we're really open about that sort of stuff, 'cause me, my Mum and my Dad and my whole family talk about it a lot. My Dad goes, "The final decision will be with you. You'll get people who will come and ask if you want to get married but you can see, and the ultimate decision will be yours." . . . In Islam, it's the final right of the woman, 'cause it's her life.

My Mum and Dad go, "The main thing in a person is the character." They might be very ugly but have a very nice personality. You're not going to get to know that just by looking at them,

are you? How can you say "yes" just by looking at them?

But it isn't really accepted to go out with a boy. I wouldn't want to hurt my parents.

You go to the person's house just to get to know them, with your family and you talk to them. I'm not saying you go out on a date. That's not how you're going to know someone, 'cause you never really know someone till you live with them.

The reason arranged marriages have been working for ages and ages now is because those women have been taking it and not speaking out against it all these years.

They were very passive, happy in the role of the weaker sex, which is not right!

In the Qur'an you have read that a man and a woman's marriage is compatible, they are companions, they fit around each other like a hand and glove . . . that the rights of the man and woman in the eyes of Allah are equal. They are on the same level, except that the man is the protector of the woman because he is physically stronger.

In the past, women didn't know about the world outside. They never experienced any of this that we're experiencing in a different environment. This is not about Islam. This is basically our culture – it's Asian culture.

What if you did whatever you consider right and you said "All right, Mother, I will marry him!" And what if you found out he wasn't right for you? What then? What would you think of your culture then?

At least I wouldn't have in mind that I'd done something wrong . . . it wouldn't have been my fault. I accepted my parents.

That's the exploiting of Islam. It's the way people interpret it. . .

(Firyal Ahmed, Manssora Awan, Shabana Begg, Saba Khan, Ferua Naz Pasha and Fozia Shah, 13 March, 1987)

EATING AND DRINKING

Being a Muslim is not just a matter of thinking and feeling but also of *doing*. Eating and drinking are the most important of all "doings" for all people, so naturally there is an Islamic view of food and drink.

It is well known that Muslims do not eat pork, although the Qur'an doesn't give the reason why Allah has forbidden it, except that it is unclean. Many Muslims today say that what this means is that pork is not a healthy meat, that it is fatty and goes "off" quickly. Certainly Muslim children develop an instinctive aversion to pork, and early in their lives it becomes a special aspect of their Muslim identity *not* to eat pork, including ham, bacon and lard.

Halal (permitted) meat is from an animal that has been slaughtered "in the name of Allah", so Muslims aren't just eating to satisfy their appetite but to raise eating to a religious act in obedience to Allah. The slaughterer is specially trained and uses a method which Muslims think will cause the animal the least amount of pain possible. Where *halal* meat is not available, devout Muslims will have a vegetarian diet or sometimes buy *kosher* meat from Jewish butchers, as the Jewish method and attitude are similar. From time to time, non-Muslims in countries such as Britain try to ban *halal* meat.

Originally, Muslims were not absolutely forbidden to drink alcohol but were simply told not to get drunk and not to pray when they had been drinking. However, some of the early Muslims didn't have enough self-control to drink in moderation, and so the Prophet had to forbid alcohol altogether. Nowadays, narcotic drugs are also against Islamic law: they didn't exist in the time of the Prophet, so they are not mentioned in the Qur'an or *hadith*. Muslim scholars say that taking drugs is *like* drinking alcohol because both affect how people think and make them lose responsibility for their actions. This is a good example of *qiyas* (analogy or comparison) and it is a way of applying the Qur'an to modern situations.

BETTING AND BOOZING

People who drink a lot of alcohol are often gamblers and people who gamble are often serious drinkers: so it seems to Islam. Anyway, the Qur'an often speaks of alcohol and gambling together, saying that they are both bad for people and they make each other worse.

You who believe, liquor and gambling, idols and raffles, are only a filthy work of Satan; avoid them so that you may prosper. Satan only wants to stir up enmity and jealousy among you by means of liquor and gambling, and to hinder you from remembering God and from praying. So will you stop?
(Qur'an 5: 90-1)

DON'T PLAY WITH YOUR FOOD!

From the eating habits of the Messenger of Allah, Muhammad, Muslims have taken several of their customs concerning food. He said, for example, that Muslims should wash their hands before and after eating, and that they should call on the name of Allah to thank him for their food and drink. It was said by Abu Huraira that the Prophet never complained about the food he ate, and if he didn't like something, he just left it! The practice Muslims have of only eating with their right hand and, in many Muslim communities, of not even giving or taking food with their left hand, can be traced to a specific piece of advice given to someone who obviously had bad table manners. It is recorded in a *hadith*:

Umar b. Abu Salama said: "I was under the care of Allah's Messenger and my hand used to pick at random in the dish, so Allah's Messenger said to me: 'Invoke the name of Allah and eat with your right [hand] and eat what is near you.' "
(Ahmad von Denffer, A *Day with the* Prophet, The Islamic Foundation, p. 41)

YOU CAN'T LEARN ON AN
EMPTY STOMACH

In many parts of Britain the meat in school dinners is not *halal* and may even be pork in some form. Muslim pupils who do not eat non-*halal* meat generally choose a vegetarian meal if this is available; but in many parts of the country it is not provided, or children at the end of the dinner queue find it has gone when they reach the hatch. There is a serious worry that the health and education of Muslim children will suffer from this situation. Bradford started offering *halal* meat as an option in the dinner provided by the school meals service. Some Muslim pupils were asked on television for their views on *halal* dinners – before and after their introduction.

We only had one choice then – only cheese – and sometimes we had fish.

We didn't used to get much choice and didn't used to like the food that much.
They [non-Muslim classmates] didn't ask us questions but they just used to say sometimes, 'Why don't you get more of this type [i.e. non-*halal*] of dinner?' And we just used to say we didn't like it. They might break the friendship. . .
'I used to only have a pudding, that's all. . . . I used to feel hungry. I didn't tell 'em [parents]. I thought I had to go hungry.
'I didn't tell my parents either coz they say I've got to pay dinner money and it costs a lot.
'I also pay dinner money, you see, and I don't like cheese so I didn't eat much, only chips when we had them or just pudding. . . . At the end of the day, I felt very hungry.'
(Pupils of a Bradford Secondary School interviewed for the Channel 4 production "Holy Meat", broadcast in August 1986)

Good food and drink are essential to festivals: both the home and the mosque are centres of Islam which cater for the whole of Muslim life, which is, in every way, a celebration of the senses.

ENJOYING LIFE AND SAYING "THANK YOU"

Self-restraint and self-denial – not doing or having what you want all the time and not doing or having certain things at all – are important aspects of Muslim behaviour. But Islam is not a

"forbidding" religion and Muslims are far from miserable. There are happy times when Muslims celebrate weddings and births, victories and gains, and the wonders of God's world in so many ways. They are more than just occasions for "having a good time" but experiences which move the sensitive Muslim to reflect on Allah's goodness and to thank and praise him for it.

In particular, there are two festivals in the Islamic calendar for enjoying and thanking.

Eid-ul-fitr comes right after the month of fasting. Muslims join in congregational prayer, if possible in an open field.

Eid-ul-adha begins on the tenth and goes on until the twelfth day of the twelfth month. It falls during the days of the pilgrimage to Makka but is celebrated by Muslims everywhere: they commemorate the Prophet Ibrahim's (Abraham) willingness to sacrifice his son Ismail (Ishmael) at Allah's command. Allah accepted Ibrahim's devotion and obedience and asked him to sacrifice a lamb instead.

After congregational prayers, Muslims who can afford it sacrifice animals like goats, sheep, cows or camels. They share the meat among their families, neighbours and the poor.

FRESH AND SALT WATER

Sometimes it is the simplest and most obvious things that give you a quick, clear, penetrating insight into life: the natural world and human nature are full of contrasts, and two opposites can *both* be good!

> Both seas are not alike: this one is sweet, fresh, refreshing to drink, while the other is salty, briny. From each you eat fresh meat and extract jewelry to wear. You see ships sailing along on it so that you may seek His bounty and so that you may feel thankful.
>
> (Qur'an 35: 12)

Whee! Eid-ul-fitr, the festival which marks the end of Ramadan, the month of fasting, is a reward that brings relief from that discipline and an overall sense of release. In front of the gateway to the Great Mosque at Fatehpur Sikri (near Agra in northern India) a ferris wheel is erected especially for this Eid. It seems right to combine the duty of communal worship with the desire for relaxation and pleasure.

THANKS FOR EVERYTHING

Nasrudin was a wandering teacher (*mulla*) of the seventeenth century. He was Master of the Dervishes, the mystical dance groups, but he is best remembered for his tongue-in-cheek stories that brought everybody down to earth.

Nasrudin, when he was in India, passed near a strange-looking building, at the entrance of which a hermit was sitting. He had an air of abstraction and calm, and Nasrudin thought that he would make some sort of contact with him. 'Surely', he thought, 'a devout philosopher like me must have something in common with this saintly individual.'

'I am a Yogi,' said the anchorite, in answer to the Mulla's question; 'and I am dedicated to the service of all living things, especially birds and fish.'

'Pray allow me to join you,' said the Mulla, 'for, as I had expected, we have something in common. I am strongly attracted to your sentiments, because a fish once saved my life.'

'How pleasurably remarkable!' said the Yogi; 'I shall be delighted to admit you to our company. For all my years of devotion to the cause of animals, I have never yet been privileged to attain such intimate communion with them as you. Saved your life! This amply substantiates our doctrine that all the animal kindom is interlinked.'

So Nasrudin sat with the Yogi for some weeks, contemplating his navel and learning various curious gymnastics.

At length the Yogi asked him: 'If you feel able, now that we are better acquainted, to communicate to me your supreme experience with the life-saving fish, I would be more than honoured.'

'I am not sure about that,' said the Mulla, 'now that I have heard more of your ideas.'

But the Yogi pressed him, with tears in his eyes, calling him 'Master' and rubbing his forehead in the dust before him.

'Very well, if you insist,' said Nasrudin, 'though I am not quite sure whether you are ready (to use your parlance) for the revelation I have to make. The fish certainly saved my life. I was on the verge of starvation when I caught it. It provided me with food for three days.'

(Idries Shah, "Saved His Life", *The Exploits of the Incomparable Nasrudin*, Pan Books Ltd, 1973, p. 64)

GIVING AND FORGIVING

Sharidan Ayub, aged 13, comes from Indonesia but is living in Britain. He loves Eid-ul-fitr because of the forgiveness – from Allah and from other Muslims – that it celebrates: he does not mind admitting that he loves Eid also for the treats.

Eid starts a month of forgiveness. In Siwal we can always give forgiveness to people and also ask for forgiveness from people, especially from our parents, relatives, friends and teachers.

On the first day of Eid, I usually get up early, clean myself which is important to a Muslim. On the first day of Eid, Muslims prefer to wear nice and good clothes which depend on their own traditions. After asking forgiveness from my parents, brothers and sisters, we all go to the mosque to pray. After that we can go to visit our relatives and our friends. But I always remember to ask my parents for my pocket money which can always be asked for on Eid in my country!

BELONGING TO THE MUSLIM COMMUNITY

The Islamic calendar dates from the year 622 CE. This is not the birth, death or important event during the life of the Prophet but the year of the *hijra* (migration). People who refused to accept Islam and resented attempts to change their corrupt ways drove the early Muslims out of Makka, threatening to kill them. Most of the Muslims escaped safely and fled to a town that came to be known as Madina. There, in freedom, Muslim life began and a community was established. The sense of belonging, caring and being responsible for each other was there from the very beginning and makes Islam a religion not for lone individuals but for a community – *ummah*.

Muslims don't see Islam as standing still but rather as a growing community which is always being extended by its own birth rate and its outreach, or mission. It must do more than survive: it must also expand.

THE ROPE OF ALLAH

If anyone was in serious trouble – drowning or being burned – and a rope was lowered to them they would grab it straight away. That is the image of God – Allah in Arabic – reaching down to help. The idea that Islam is a community-based religion means that by clinging to each other and clinging to Allah's rope Islam is a relationship to Allah and a relationship to other Muslims.

> Cling firmly together by means of God's rope, and do not be divided. Remember God's favour towards you when you were enemies; He united your hearts so that you became brothers because of His favour. You were on the brink of a fiery pit, and He saved you from it. Thus, God explains His signs to you, so that you may be guided.
> Let there be a community among you who will invite [others] to [do] good, command what is proper and forbid what is improper; those will be prosperous. Do not be like those who split up and disagreed after explanations had come to them; those will have awful torment!
> (Qur'an 3: 102-5)

THE LAST TRICK

An essential ingredient of *ummah* is openness: it is not enough to know simply that there are other Muslims or even to be with other Muslims – it is vital that Muslims respect and trust each other. The *Gulistan* of Sadi, written over 700 years ago, contains many stories about human relationships: this one is about power and protection.

> Once a wrestler had become the master of his art; he knew three-hundred-and-sixty-five wrestling tricks and could show a fresh trick every day throughout the year. He was particularly fond of one of his students and taught him all that he knew except one trick. With the passage of time the youth became proficient in the art of wrestling and none of his contemporaries could match his skill and ability. One day, the young wrestler boasted before the King: "Any superiority my teacher has over me is purely due to his seniority; otherwise, I am not

Once a paradise for Muslim and Jewish culture, Catholic Spain expelled her Jews and Muslims in 1492. But today, a need for the resources of Arab countries, a respect for the power of Islam and a new spirit of understanding have made it possible for mosques to be built again in Spain. The "Arab Mosque" near Marbella on the south coast is in frequent use and re-affirms the idea of Islam as an international chain of loyalty.

inferior in power, and am his equal in skill." The young man's lack of respect displeased the King. He ordered a wrestling match to be held. The ministers of state, nobles of the court, and gallant men assembled to watch, the youth struck the master first. The master, being aware that the youth was his superior in strength, engaged him in the last trick which the master had not taught him. The young man could not get out of the clutch of the master. He seized him with both hands and, lifting him bodily from the ground, raised him above his head and threw him on the ground. The crowd stood up and cheered. The King ordered that the master be given a great reward and grand robes. The King said to the young man: "You played the traitor with your own master but failed in your rash attempt to defeat him." The youth replied, "O King! My master did not overcome me by strength and ability, but by one cunning trick which he did not teach me." The master said, "I reserved the trick for such a day as this. Have you not heard the wise say, 'Do not give your friend so much power that, if he turned against you, he could do you serious injury.' "

(Ashraf Abu Turab and Zia Sardar, eds., A *Time to Speak*: *Anecdotes from Sadi Shirazi*, The Islamic Foundation, 1980, pp. 27-8).

COMPULSORY UNITY

In the broken world we live in today, Muslims are aware of the need for unity as never before. Sermons are often based on the need for cooperation and generosity, and the *imam* (leader) will draw from the Qur'an or *hadith* to support the points he makes. This sermon was given at the time of an oil summit when Muslim Heads of State were meeting, and the idea of harmony was very much in their minds.

Unity is fundamental to Islam. Take prayer for example. The reward for performing prayer is much more when you pray in congregation — twenty seven times more. The aim of congregational prayer is that Muslims mix together and meet each other, discuss their problems and try to help each other in finding solutions for them.

The Prophet, peace be on him, warned the Muslim ummah against being divided among itself. He ordered Muslims to be united and stand together against any outside threat. He said that the work of satan is only possible on individuals but not on groups, meaning that satan does his best to misguide and seduce the individual but his machinations do not affect groups.

One day the Prophet, peace be on him, saw travellers who had left their caravans to take rest having travelled for a long time and they looked as if they did not know each other. So he commented, "It is satan who divided you among yourselves." The travellers took his advice and closed ranks and worked more closely together. In Islam, unity is compulsory and should be given greater priority. . . .

The same lesson is found in the story of a wise old man who wanted to give advice to his sons before he died. He asked one of them to break one stick which was easily done. But when he asked them to break a bundle of sticks, they could not. The lesson was clear: strength lies in unity.

Disputes and conflicts in today's Muslim ummah divert attention from the main issues and from the real threats. May God grant us the wisdom to be able to identify what these issues and threats are. We will certainly be successful if we follow the Qur'an and the Sunnah of the Prophet, peace be on him.

(An extract from the Friday *khutbah* (sermon) by Shaykh Hamid Khalifa at the London Central Mosque on 17 January, 1987)

GOING ON PILGRIMAGE TO MAKKA

Pilgrimage – *hajj* in Arabic – is one of the five pillars of Islam, those practices which are central to Islam and are its central support.

Hajj generally means setting out with a definite purpose and actually refers to going on pilgrimage to Makka, a town in Saudi Arabia. Every Muslim – male and female – is expected to go on *hajj* at least once in their life unless they are too ill or they can't afford it. There's a set time for the *hajj*: it's during the twelfth month of the Islamic calendar.

The *hajjis* and *hajjas* (male and female pilgrims) have a strong sense of oneness and togetherness.

The Ka'ba (cube) is the focal point of Makka. Said to be originally an altar to Allah built by Adam, the first prophet, it deteriorated over the centuries into a house of idols. It was the last prophet, Muhammad, who removed all the idols from inside and restored the Ka'ba as a place of worship to the one God. Encircling the Ka'ba

It doesn't matter how the pilgrims come to Saudi Arabia – by land, air or sea. It only matters that they come. The city of Makka itself is not on the coast and has no airport or railway station. It is approached by road – by car, coach or camel, or even on foot.

On hajj, unity inside needs unity outside: the ihram, the two pieces of unsewn white cloth worn by men and the plain cotton dresses worn by women, expresses the solidarity of society and the simplicity of the spirit.

seven times is the key ritual of the *hajj*.

Another very important experience for Muslims takes place around the hill of Arafat, about 25 km from Makka. On the ninth day of the month, all the *hajjis* and *hajjas* spend the afternoon in prayer together, perhaps 2 million in all. Muslims say that Adam was reconciled with Eve, his wife, at Arafat, and it is known that the Prophet gave his farewell speech there. He once said that the best of prayers is the prayer on the day of Arafat.

GOING ROUND IN CIRCLES . . .

Going on pilgrimage to Makka is not just a duty for Muslims but also an opportunity for them to thank Allah for all they have and to express that thanks by ritual and good deeds.

Thus We settled Abraham at the site of the House, [saying]: "Do not associate anything with Me; and purify My house for those who walk around it, and those who stand there [praying], and those who bow and kneel down with their foreheads on the ground [in worship]. Proclaim the Pilgrimage among mankind: they will come to you on foot and on every lean beast [of burden]; let them come from every deep gully, to bear witness to the advantages they have, and to mention God's name on appointed days over such heads of livestock as He has provided them with. Then eat some of it and feed the needy pauper. Then let them attend to their grooming, fulfil their vows, and let them circle round the Ancient House."
(Qur'an 22: 26-9)

OUTSIDE, INSIDE

What the pilgrims *do* matters, but so does what they think and feel. Inner preparation and discipline – and the inner journey itself – are themes which appear quite often in Sufi stories such as this one.

A certain Kalandar on his travels fell in with the sage Kadudar, and asked him the question which had been puzzling him for many years:

'Why do you forbid your followers to make the pilgrimage? How can man forbid what has been commanded from On High?'

Kadudar, whose name means 'possessor of the gourd', held up a dried gourd and said:

'Can you forbid this pumpkin to be a pumpkin? Nobody can forbid the fulfilling of a celestial command; so that even if a man appeared to do so, in reality it would be impossible.

'The duty of the Guide, however, is to ensure that pilgrimages are not performed by people in an unsuitable inner state, just as the guardians of the Sanctuary will prevent anyone from carrying out the pilgrimage rites in an unsuitable outward state.

'All pilgrimage has an outward and inward aspect. The ordinary man will help the pilgrim when he needs money or food, and will raise him up if he has collapsed on the road. The Man of the Path, minutely discerning similar necessities in the inner life, is compelled to give his aid in his own way.'

(Idries Shah, "Kadudar and the Pilgrimage", *Thinkers of the East*, Penguin, 1971, p. 24)

FROM MAKKA WITH LOVE

Dr Nagis Khan is a Muslim doctor, originally from Pakistan but now living in Britain. In a personal interview, she describes what going on *hajj* meant to her and how she felt when she reached the Ka'ba for the first time in her life.

I felt that it was a good time in my life as I was going on to a profession where I would come across a lot of sick people who would benefit from Allah through me.

As soon as you see that, the feeling is really something that a Muslim cannot describe because you just want to cry because you have waited so long to come to that place and when you see that, your feeling is really something that words cannot describe. Then when you have got control of yourself, you go near it and you have to do certain prayers which I did like everyone else, and say certain prayers which I did. Then I did get a chance to kiss the stone which was again something – as soon as you kiss the stone you feel a tremendous amount of peace which I have never felt before.

The whole concept of *hajj* is that when you go for *hajj* you leave all your material things behind and you stand in the presence of God. It is the same as it will be on the Day of Judgement, so therefore, on the Day of Judgement there are going to be lots and lots of people but you will be relating to Allah on your own and it is the same feeling. There are lots of people around you but you have nothing to do with them. You are alone and there is God with you. You talk to him directly and he answers.

You cannot describe or measure spirituality but it certainly made a lot of difference. . . . I felt that I really needed God once I had made the pilgrimage and it was a very strong feeling.

GOING TO THE MOSQUE

Wherever a Muslim bows in prayer to Allah is a mosque. The Arabic word *masjid* means a place where the head touches the ground. It can be any clean place, or anywhere that a prayer rug can be put down – any room, the roadside, an airport, a factory, the desert. . .

Muslims need to pray together as well as to meet socially, to study and discuss communal matters. So Muslim communities build a mosque, or occasionally they will convert a disused building into a mosque. The main room is a prayer hall which has no furniture; it may be decorated, but never with pictures of people. The *qibla* (direction) wall points worshippers towards Makka: it is marked by the *mihrab*, a niche or panel which stands out against the plain wall or other decoration. Beside the *mihrab* there is usually a *minbar*, a pulpit with steps. From there the *imam* (leader) delivers a *khutbah* (sermon), especially on Fridays at noon.

Going to the mosque is the way Muslims can express the idea of *ummah* and engage fully in Islamic life.

BETTER THAN SPORT OR BUSINESS!

Friday is a special day of congregation for Muslims but the same ideas and feelings apply to all prayer-times. It is on Friday that Muslims try especially hard to offer their midday prayers in the mosque, so as to be with as many other Muslims as possible, but actually Muslims prefer to offer their set prayers in company every time.

> You who believe, when [the call to] prayer is announced on the day of Congregation, hasten to remember God and stop trading. That will be better for you if you only realized it.
> Once prayer has been performed, then disperse throughout the land and seek God's bounty. Remember God often so that you may prosper. Yet whenever they see some business or some sport, they flock towards it and leave you standing there [alone].
> SAY: "What God has is better than any sport or business. God is the best Provider!"
> (Qur'an 62: 9-11)

WHEN IS A SERMON NOT A SERMON?

Mulla Nasrudin was always in great demand as a story-teller and preacher, but he wanted people to be able to think for themselves, too, and he was often very unconventional. He wanted to convey the idea that life itself is a sermon, that you can overhear wisdom as easily in the marketplace as in the mosque.

> One day the villagers thought they would play a joke on Nasrudin. As he was supposed to be a holy man of some indefinable sort, they went to him and asked him to preach a sermon in their mosque. He agreed.
> When the day came, Nasrudin mounted the pulpit and spoke:
> 'O people! Do you know what I am going to tell you?'
> 'No, we do not know,' they cried.

'Until you know, I cannot say. You are too ignorant to make a start on,' said the Mulla, overcome with indignation that such ignorant people should waste his time. He descended from the pulpit and went home.

Slightly chagrined, a deputation went to his house again, and asked him to preach the following Friday, the day of prayer.

Nasrudin started his sermon with the same question as before.

This time the congregation answered, as one man:

'Yes, we know.'

'In that case,' said the Mulla, 'there is no need for me to detain you longer. You may go.' And he returned home.

Having been prevailed upon to preach for the third Friday in succession, he started his address as before:

'Do you know or do you not?'

The congegation was ready.

'Some of us do, and others do not.'

'Excellent,' said Nasrudin, 'then let those who know communicate their knowledge to those who do not.'

And he went home.

(Idries Shah, "The Sermon of Nasrudin", *The Exploits of the Incomparable Mulla Nasrudin*, Pan Books Ltd, 1973, p. 44)

THE HUB OF THE WHEEL

The role of the mosque has gone full circle: in the days of the Prophet it was a community centre, but for centuries in many countries it existed only for prayer and religious study. Now it is a community centre once again. For example, since the Islamic revival (revolution) in Iran in the early 1970s, the mosque has fulfilled a range of roles.

The mosque was vital to the outcome of the Iranian revolution. . . . Khomeini often refers to the mosque as a "sangar", or bulwark, a bastion of good against internal or external enemies. . . .

Among what would seem to be the more secular functions of the Iranian mosque today is the issue of "kupon", the ration cards for basic foodstuffs and supplies that have been introduced since the revolution. . . . The mosque is becoming increasingly important as a supervisory body in official appointments, particularly for voluntary work in rural areas. Committees of mullahs attached to the local mosque, revolutionary guards and members of the local "komitehs" vet candidates and pronounce on whether they are "maktabi", the name given to those who follow the regime's religious line. . . .

The mosque is an obvious centre for charitable work. The deeply rooted custom of "nazr", a religious vow conditional upon the favourable outcome of an examination, illness or other personal uncertainty, often takes the form of a "sofreh", or spread. The person fulfilling the "nazr" pays for food which is distributed by the mosque to the needy, or simply to anyone who happens to be in the mosque at the time. . . .

Iran has long been famous for its mosques. . . . However, many of these had become mere tourist attractions, beautiful but empty works of architecture whose original purpose had atrophied. Today, with humbler mosques from later periods, they are once again serving as focal points for their communities, centres for collective worship and much else besides.

("Iran's Mosques Tighten Grip", *Arabia: The Islamic World Review*, February 1982, p. 14)

Few people feel they need police protection to say their prayers, but racist groups in the East End of London had been harassing the Muslim community so much that going to the mosque became an act of faith and bravado — not only a religious duty but also a political statement.

WASHING BEFORE PRAYER

Muslims cannot suddenly start praying just because it's time: they have to get into the right frame of mind, feeling that Allah is "high" and they are "low". This needs mental preparation, a few quiet moments to create calm and commitment to prayer. It also needs physical preparation: Muslims get the body ready by special washing routines, at least once a day. This is called *wuzu*, and it's all part of worship, not an optional extra.

Wuzu must be done with pure running water (cold, warm or hot) such as from a tap or fountain. At home, Muslims may stand at a washbasin or perch on the edge of the bath-tub to do this, but mosques will have special fittings, such as rows of taps which run into gulleys and solid, fixed

There are many times when Muslims feel the disciplines of their religion are a real delight. They do what Allah has directed and also realise that there are personal and social benefits. At noon, on a dry, dusty day in the height of the summer in Sudan, wuzu in a fountain of clear, cool water in a marble courtyard is sheer ecstasy!

stools beside them for Muslims to sit on safely and comfortably.

Wuzu means that even in hot, dry countries Muslims put a lot of emphasis on hygiene and have clean habits that show consideration for other people as well as personal purity. Cleanliness isn't separate from their religion: it's actually built into it.

WET AND DRY CLEANING

Certain experiences and situations – such as sexual intercourse or going to the toilet – make a Muslim *junub*, that is, not in the right state to offer prayer. Even so, the Qur'an expresses a realistic and understanding view: if there is no fresh water available, the ritual can be performed with sand.

If you are soiled, take a full bath. If you are ill or on a journey, or one of you has just come from the closet or had any contact with women, and you do not find any water, then resort to wholesome soil and wipe your faces and hands with some of it.

God does not want to place any inconvenience on you, but He does want to purify you and to complete His favour towards you, in order that you may be grateful.
(Qur'an 5: 6)

DO AS THEY DO

The command *to* wash before prayer is recorded in the Qur'an but it is from the *hadith* that Muslims find out *how* to wash – from the example of The Prophet and Sunnis. Doing as they do brings a Muslim into deeper contact with the Islamic tradition.

Humran reported that 'Uthman (may Allah be

pleased with him) called for ablution water and washed his hands thrice. He then rinsed his mouth and cleaned his nose with water. He then washed his face three times, then washed his right arm up to the elbow three times, then washed his left arm like that, then wiped his head; then washed his right foot up to the ankle (three times), then washed his left foot like that, and then said, I saw the Messenger of Allah (peace and blessings of Allah be upon him) performing ablution like this ablution of mine.'
(Abdul Hamid Siddique, *Selection from Hadith*, 11, Islamic Book Publishers, p. 8)

INDECENCY AND DISEASE

Perhaps cleanliness is next to Godliness; at least, next to goodliness. . . . In a newsletter from a mosque to its members and visitors, *wuzu* is discussed in relation to sexual diseases. In this view, impurity exists on many levels and so does cleansing.

Purity amongst other things is a fundamental characteristic of a Muslim who is committed to his belief. It manifests itself in his every action, whether purely religious or mundane since every good thought or action done for the sake of Allah is considered worship.

Purity in the realm of the physical and material aspects of life is incumbent on [obligatory to] every Muslim. The best example of this is a Muslim's Salat. We are required to make ablutions perhaps five times a day. Could this leave any blemish on those parts of the body which is thus cleansed? It is reported in a hadith in which Rasulullah says: "Can you inform me if there is a stream running in front of your door and you wash in it five times a day, would this leave any dirt on your bodies?" The companions replied no! So Rasulullah said, "It is similar to the Prayer by which you are purified." Reflecting on this hadith, we find there is a link between physical purity and spiritual purity.

To illustrate further, a Muslim is on occasion required to have a complete bath to purify himself from natural functions in order to engage himself in the spiritual domain. This is the required purity for a Muslim in relation to his Creator. Our relations with all creation should be based on this principle of purity. It is therefore imperative that on every level the basis of our relations should stem from Purity. Socially we should remove all impurity such as cheating, deception, malice, evil thought and the like, because it is against the principle of purity.
(Islamic Cultural Centre, London NW8, Newsletter No. 25, February 1987)

PRAYING

Salah – prayer – is the second pillar of Islam, so it is something Muslims really have to do, but it is also supposed to be a beautiful experience, sometimes soothing, sometimes challenging. Muslims don't pray just in the head or in the heart but with their bodies, too: it is physical as well as spiritual. Because Islam is a socially-based religion, Muslims try to pray with others but even when they can't they will use the words and movements other Muslims use and not go their own way. They can, of course, always add personal prayers at any time; this is called du'a.

Salah has a definite form of words and order of movements called a rak'ah. Muslims pray five times a day – a varying number of rak'ahs – so they never go very long without thinking about Allah and of the good life they should live. Prayer is not separate from everyday life but woven into it.

Muslim children start to learn the rak'ahs when they are quite young and by the time they are about 12, when they join in with the adults, they should be able to do them perfectly.

KEEP IT UP!

Like so many things in life, Islam says, prayer needs to be worked at to get it right: practice makes perfect!

God's guidance means (real) guidance. We have been ordered to commit ourselves to live in peace with the Lord of the Universe: "Keep up prayer and heed Him! He is the One before Whom you will be summoned."
(Qur'an 6: 71-2)

NEITHER WITHIN NOR WITHOUT

Shamsi Tabriz was a wandering dervish of the thirteenth century. The group he was part of used dance, meditation and other means of reaching perfection in worship, which they saw as being completely inside oneself. Shamsi Tabriz thought of this as reaching a place, the ancient word which he described in this way:

There comes a Sound, from neither within nor without,

From neither right nor left, from neither behind nor in front,
From neither below nor above, from neither East nor West,
Nor is it of the elements: water, air, fire, earth, and the like;
From where then? It is from that place thou art in search of;
Turn ye toward the place wherefrom the Lord makes His appearance.
From where a restless fish out of water gets water to live in,

From the place where the prophet Moses saw
  the divine Light,
From the place where the fruits get their ripening
  influence,
From the place where the stones get transmuted
  to gems,
From the place to which even an infidel turns in
  distress,

From the place to which all men turn when they
  find this world a vale of tears.
It is not given to us to describe such a blessed
  place;
It is a place where even the heretics would leave
  off their heresies.

(Ira Friedlander, *The Whirling Dervishes*, Wildwood
House, 1975, pp. 201)

Any passer-by can see this woman at prayer on the pavement: she has unrolled her prayer mat, arranged her prayer beads, covered her head and neck in a shawl, and is preparing herself by reciting some verses of the Qur'an. She does not speak, and in the silence she offers to Allah no one can see what is happening inside her, what she is feeling, thinking and sensing in the spirit. Islam can be very public, but it also lives in the private relationship between each Muslim and Allah.

SUMMER DAYS, WINTER NIGHTS . . .

In temperate regions like Britain, there is a very big difference between the length of the days and nights in summer and winter. Most people's daily routine goes by the clock not by the "light", so Muslims need to have the prayer times worked out and printed so that they can keep a copy at home or work, or carry it with them. It is inconvenient, but many Muslims in Britain say that at least they do not pray out of sheer habit at a particular time but because they have made themselves aware of the need to be alert to the passing of time. The June and December pages of prayer times in Britain in 1987 show the greatest disparity in time.

	JUNE							DECEMBER				
Date	(Fajr) Dawn	Sunrise	(Zuhr) Noon	(Asr) Afternoon	(Maghrib) Sunset	(Isha) Evening	Date	(Fajr) Dawn	Sunrise	(Zuhr) Noon	(Asr) Afternoon	(Maghrib) Sunset	(Isha) Evening
1	2.43	4.49	12.59	5.19	9.10	11.07	1	5.43	7.43	11.51	2.00	3.56	5.50
2	2.42	4.48	1.00	5.19	9.11	11.08	2	5.44	7.44	11.51	2.00	3.56	5.50
3	2.40	4.48	1.00	5.20	9.12	11.09	3	5.45	7.46	11.51	2.00	3.55	5.49
4	2.39	4.47	1.00	5.20	9.13	11.11	4	5.46	7.47	11.52	2.00	3.55	5.49
5	2.38	4.46	1.00	5.21	9.14	11.13	5	5.47	7.48	11.52	2.00	3.54	5.49
6	2.37	4.46	1.00	5.21	9.15	11.14	6	5.48	7.49	11.53	2.00	3.54	5.49
7	2.36	4.45	1.00	5.22	9.16	11.15	7	5.49	7.51	11.53	2.01	3.54	5.49
8	2.35	4.45	1.01	5.22	9.16	11.16	8	5.50	7.52	11.53	2.01	3.54	5.48
9	2.34	4.44	1.01	5.22	9.17	11.17	9	5.51	7.53	11.54	2.01	3.53	5.48
10	2.33	4.44	1.01	5.23	9.18	11.18	10	5.52	7.54	11.54	2.01	3.53	5.48
11	2.32	4.43	1.01	5.23	9.19	11.19	11	5.53	7.55	11.55	2.01	3.53	5.48
12	2.32	4.43	1.01	5.23	9.20	11.20	12	5.54	7.56	11.55	2.02	3.53	5.49
13	2.31	4.43	1.02	5.24	9.20	11.20	13	5.54	7.57	11.56	2.02	3.53	5.49
14	2.31	4.43	1.02	5.24	9.21	11.20	14	5.55	7.58	11.56	2.02	3.53	5.49
15	2.30	4.43	1.02	5.24	9.21	11.21	15	5.56	7.59	11.57	2.02	3.53	5.49
16	2.30	4.42	1.02	5.25	9.22	11.21	16	5.57	7.59	11.57	2.02	3.53	5.49
17	2.29	4.42	1.02	5.25	9.22	11.22	17	5.57	8.00	11.58	2.02	3.54	5.50
18	2.29	4.42	1.03	5.25	9.23	11.23	18	5.58	8.01	11.58	2.02	3.54	5.50
19	2.28	4.42	1.03	5.26	9.23	11.24	19	5.59	8.02	11.59	2.02	3.54	5.50
20	2.28	4.43	1.03	5.26	9.24	11.25	20	5.59	8.02	11.59	2.02	3.55	5.51
21	2.28	4.43	1.03	5.26	9.24	11.25	21	6.00	8.03	12.00	2.02	3.55	5.51
22	2.28	4.43	1.04	5.26	9.24	11.25	22	6.00	8.03	12.00	2.03	3.56	5.52
23	2.29	4.43	1.04	5.27	9.24	11.26	23	6.01	8.04	12.01	2.03	3.56	5.52
24	2.30	4.43	1.04	5.27	9.24	11.26	24	6.01	8.04	12.01	2.04	3.57	5.53
25	2.30	4.44	1.04	5.27	9.25	11.26	25	6.01	8.04	12.02	2.04	3.58	5.54
26	2.31	4.44	1.04	5.27	9.25	11.26	26	6.02	8.05	12.02	2.05	3.58	5.54
27	2.32	4.45	1.05	5.27	9.25	11.26	27	6.02	8.05	12.03	2.06	3.59	5.55
28	2.33	4.45	1.05	5.27	9.24	11.26	28	6.02	8.05	12.03	2.06	4.00	5.56
29	2.33	4.46	1.05	5.27	9.24	11.25	29	6.03	8.05	12.04	2.07	4.01	5.57
30	2.34	4.46	1.05	5.27	9.24	11.25	30	6.03	8.05	12.04	2.07	4.02	5.57
							31	6.03	8.05	12.05	2.08	4.03	5.58

(Timetable for prayers in London, Islamic Cultural Centre, London NW8)

READING THE QUR'AN

Muslims treat the Qur'an with the utmost respect. They wrap it in a beautiful cloth and place it on a high place in a bookshelf at home to show that it is "above" all other writings, or else it is kept in a place by itself, showing that it is in a class of its own.

There are certain rules about what can and can't be done while the Qur'an is being read. For example, both men and women must be modestly dressed; they don't touch the Qur'an until they have done their *wuzu*, as they do before praying; they only read the Qur'an in a clean place, and no other book can be put on top of it. During a public recitation, or when an individual Muslim is reading privately, Muslims must not eat, drink, smoke or have any physical contact.

The Qur'an is often placed on an X-shaped stand or low stool so that it can be opened safely. A Muslim sits cross-legged in front of it and chants clearly – the Qur'an must be heard as well as read.

Quite young Muslim children learn to recite the Qur'an by heart: someone who has memorized the entire Qur'an is given the title *hafiz*.

FIRST CALL

One of the best reasons a Muslim could ever have for reading the Qur'an is that it is itself the record of what the prophet Muhammad read. Although he was illiterate, he was able to read what the angel showed him – a copy of the Qur'an which exists in heaven.

> Read in the name of your Lord who creates,
> creates man from a clot!
> Read, for your Lord is most Generous,
> Who teaches by means of the pen,
> teaches man what he does not know.
> However man is so arrogant,
> for he sees himself as self-sufficient,
> Yet to your Lord will be the Return.
> (Qur'an 96: 1-8)

DAWN IS NIGHT AND DAY

Muslims believe that it is always good to read the Qur'an, but at certain times and places or in certain situations of your life you get more out of it – especially at turning points. Tirmidhi, one of the "accurate six", recorded this *hadith* about the best time of the day to read the Qur'an:

> Abu Huraira said that the Prophet said about Allah's word [Qur'an 17:78]: [The recital of] the Qur'an at dawn is always witnessed – the angels of the night and the angels of the day witness it.
> (Ahmad von Denffer, *A Day with the Prophet*, The Islamic Foundation, 1979, p. 32)

Perhaps for information, perhaps for instruction, perhaps for inspiration . . . this Muslim has shut out the everyday world around him and has immersed himself in reading the Qur'an. He is totally absorbed by the words revealed by Allah.

FROM ME TO YOU

When a revolution broke out in Iraq in 1958, Mohammad Fadhel Jamali was among those arrested and tried by the Special High Military Tribunal. He was fined, imprisoned and condemned to death. He described how he waited for over a year and a half under sentence of death, waiting for execution or release. Eventually, his death sentence was commuted and after three years he was set free. Fadhel is one of those people who, in coming close to death, *have* come closer to life: he said he felt as though he had travelled to another world and returned like a newborn baby to the world of the living. In prison he wrote regularly to his son, Abbas, expressing many of his views on life. On one occasion he wrote about the value of reading the Qur'an.

Baghdad, February 10, 1961

Dear Abbas,

After presenting you my good greetings, I pray for your safety, success and guidance.

I thank you for your letter dated January 25 in which you inform me about your examinations in chemistry and mathematics, and tell me that you seek help by reading the Koran and depending on Allah. All these items are cheerful news. As for my comments on your letter, in great brevity they are as follows:

(1) My view is that all life is an examination and that Allah created man in order to examine him in this world. Every one of us has to pass an examination every hour and every day of his life in every act which he performs. We must therefore do our best and work well to succeed in life. Success is required not only in mathematics and chemistry but in everything, and we must seek the help of the Holy Koran every day for success in the examinations of life.

(2) You describe the effect of your reading the Holy Koran as soothing, and reassuring to the self, and I say that the Holy Koran is 'light, guidance, counsel, mercy, and a cure for inner troubles.'

(Mohammed Fadhel Jamali, *Letters on Islam Written by a Father in Prison to his Son*, The World of Islam Festival Trust, 1978, p. 3)

GIVING CHARITY

For the Muslim, Allah can be worshipped indirectly as well as directly – that is, by loving other people.

The Arabic word zakat is quite hard to translate: sometimes it is "poor due", but the charity doesn't go only to poor people. It isn't quite like giving to charity because it doesn't happen on the spur of the moment and, anyway, Muslims are supposed to pay it. It isn't quite like taxes because it isn't deducted by the Government from what you earn. Perhaps it's best translated as "charity tax".

Zakat is based on the idea that whatever people have doesn't really belong to them but to Allah: people do things, not on their own but because Allah is helping them. What we own is held in trust from Allah. Giving zakat is an obligation to help others and to promote good causes. Because zakat suggests purity, Muslims believe that giving this money isn't just good for the people who get it, it's also good for the people who give it. It's like praying with their purse, and it makes real human beings out of them.

The amount Muslims are expected to give is 2½ per cent of their savings in cash (plus cattle and crops at different rates). In Muslim countries Muslims are pressurized to give zakat, and it is collected every year. In non-Muslim countries they can pay zakat straight to the person or group who needs it, or to an organized charity. It is up to the Muslims themselves to remember to pay their zakat and gently to remind each other.

HAVES AND HAVE-NOTS

There is a broad range of people who can receive zakat. Not all are financially poor as such, but many may be undergoing some crisis or experiencing a temporary problem of some kind. Islam realizes that sometimes people who are financially poor are rich in other ways – for example, those who are becoming Muslim may be suffering discrimination for their decision but they have an inner satisfaction.

> Charity [is meant] only for the poor, the needy, those working at [collecting and distributing] it, those [possible converts] whose hearts are being reconciled [to yours], for [freeing] captives and debtors, and [in fighting] in God's way, and for the wayfarer, as a duty imposed by God. God is Aware, Wise.
>
> (Qur'an 9: 60)

THE SNAKE

Sahih Al-Bukhari recorded a hadith about the guilt that comes from not paying the zakat:

> Abu Hurairah reported that the Messenger of Allah (peace and blessings of Allah be upon him) said: He who has been granted wealth by Allah and he did not pay his Zakat, his wealth will be personified in the form of a bald snake (bald due to the excess of poison) on the day of Resurrection having two black spots (over his eyes). The snake will coil (round his neck) on the Day of Resurrection then, catching both sides of his mouth will say: I am your money I am your accumulated wealth.
>
> (Abdul Hamid Siddique, Selection from Hadith, 75, Islamic Book Publishers, 1983, p. 41)

Thanking Allah for the gifts of health and happiness helps Muslims to reach out to others and to want to fill their needs. There is no shame in needing help and no pride in giving, for everyone — whether lepers like these in Mali or the destitutes of Western cities — has something to offer as well as to receive.

PLEASE GIVE GENEROUSLY

The Islamic community in Britain faces shortages in buildings for worship and study, and in trained

plan is to build a mosque and a *madrassah*, a Qur'anic school. A series of appeal letters has gone out to the Muslim community by post, by hand and by the "please take one" method. This extract states the case for giving "in the way of Allah".

The Islamic Education Trust . . . is in its 5th year of existence. By the Grace of Almighty ALLAH, this short period of 5 years has passed most successfully. The appropriateness of the location in the midst of a dense Muslim population, generated overwhelming support from the community. At the moment our main activities are focused around the Mosque, Madrassah, Youth project and the creation of an Islamic reference unit. The scope for expansion is tremendous and Insha' Allah we would do our best to respond to the needs of Muslim communities. In doing so, the Holy Qur'an shall be our constitution and Shariah shall be our guidelines.

The proposed plan covers the area of approximately 2,500 sq. ft., and consists of a spacious prayer hall to accomodate more than 1,000 people at a time, ablution facilities, classrooms for Islamic teachings, meeting rooms and other modern amenities. It is imperative that the construction should go on and be completed without delay. This is possible, Insha' Allah, with the generous donations and contributions from all of us.

We therefore, APPEAL most sincerely to all our fellow brothers and sisters to come forward to give us the helping hand, DONATE MOST GENEROUSLY AND ASSIST US FINANCIALLY IN THIS NOBLE TASK. There could be no more better opportunity to utilise our wealth and earnings but for the extraordinary cause of our Din. Your most valuable contribution would be acknowledged gracefully. May Allah bless us all. Aameen.

teachers. So a Trust has been set up in a British city to collect funds and embark upon building projects: the community has been using makeshift accommodation which is now too small and was never really suitable anyway. The

SHOWING KINDNESS AND ACTING FAIRLY

Ibadah (worship) is made up of two parts: *iman* (faith) and *sadakah* (justice and mercy). Muslims are encouraged to support other people – by giving food, clothing and shelter to the poor and needy; by being generous with their time and their inner selves as much as their possessions; by helping someone along the way; by showing kindness and working for justice.

Zakat is a simple payment that is necessary for everyone to survive but there is more to goodness and giving than that. *Sadakah* goes on all year round and cannot be measured in percentages. It is being warm and thoughtful; it means putting other people first no matter how much it takes; it involves making sure that no one has too much until everyone has enough; it is a matter of all pulling together and not pulling against each other; it is always seeing the best in other people and helping to make that even better; it is what makes a household into a family and a school into a community.

FOR GOD'S SAKE

Muslims believe that it is possible to show love to people you do not know because you love God and they are loved by God. Such love has its own reward and is not done for thanks.

> **They offer food to the needy, the orphan and the captive out of love for Him: "We are only feeding you for God's sake. We want no reward from you nor any thanks."**
> (Qur'an 76: 8-9)

During the hajj, after the day at Arafat, pilgrims make their way to Mina and spend two or three nights there. Nearby, at Jamrah, they perform ramyee, the act of throwing stones at three pillars. These baetyls represent the devil and, when hurling rocks at them, the pilgrims recall that the devil tempted Ismail the son of Ibrahim three times and each time he threw stones at it to drive it away. In repeating this act Muslims are symbolizing that they, too, are rejecting all forms of evil, both in society and within themselves. Many of them make a personal commitment then that they will drive bad thoughts out of their mind and never do anything they know is wrong.

THE SULTAN'S RECOVERY

This story by Sadi Shirazi shows how even very cruel people can be moved to kindness by others and that the dignity of those in a weak position can inspire a sense of justice. The Sultan recovered in more ways than one!

Once a Sultan of Khurasan was afflicted by a shocking disease. A panel of doctors saw him and decided that he could not be cured unless a young man of a particular description were sacrificed. Orders were issued to find such a man and a country-wide search was launched. At last, a farmer's son fitting the description was found. The Sultan sent for the mother and father of the youth, whose consent he obtained by giving them large property and much gold, then he turned to the Magistrate, who immediately issued a decree that the life of an ordinary man can be sacrificed to save the life of a King. When the executioner stood ready to slay the young man, he looked towards the heavens and smiled. "Why do you smile at this hour?", asked the Sultan in amazement. "Children look to their father and mother to take care of them," replied the youth. "If the parents are cruel, the *Qadi* (Judge) is called upon to punish them. A final request for justice is made to the Sultan. But in my case, the parents have agreed to give my life for worldly treasures; the Magistrate as an obedient servant of the King has sanctioned my execution; and the Sultan thinks that he will get his life by taking mine. Now I have no other refuge except Allah, the Almighty, the Just."

The Sultan was visibly moved at these words. "It is better for me," he thought, "to die than live with the help of his innocent blood." He then embraced the youth and freed him and gave him great wealth. It is related that the Sultan began to recover from that very moment and was well again within a week.

(Ashraf Abu Turab and Zia Sarder (eds.), *A Time to Speak: Anecdotes from Sadi Shirazi*, The Islamic Foundation, 1980, pp. 19-20)

"WHEN WILL IT COME, THE DAY?"

Mahmud Abu Radj, aged 12, lives in an Arab village in Israel. He sees the fighting between Arabs and Jews as a family battle: Jews and Arabs are both descendants of Ibrahim (Abraham) through his two sons, Ismail (Ishmael) and Isaac (the father of Jacob, later called Israel). Mahmud longs for peace to come and for the two to be real brothers again.

When will peace take over?
When will it come, the day,
When with armies and bombs will they do away
When all this hostility cease,
A day on which battleships
Will become palaces of leisure and fun
Floating on the seas.

A day on which the steel of guns
Will be melted into pleasure cars;
A day on which generals will begin to raise
   flowers.

When peace
Will include all the peoples of these
   neighbouring lands,
When Ishmael and Israel
Will go hand in hand,
And when every Jew —
The Arab's brother will be.
When will it come, the day?

(Jacob Zim, (ed.) *My Shalom, My Peace: Paintings and Poems by Jewish and Arab Children*, Sabra Books, 1975, p. 78)

FASTING

Unless you can imagine what it's like to be really hungry you'll never understand what starvation is like and you'll never do anything about famine. Fasting is a means of systematic sympathy: by not eating or drinking during daylight hours throughout the Islamic month of Ramadan every year, Muslims can empathize with those who are not fasting but starving.

There are other reasons for fasting – it gives Muslims self-discipline and enough flexibility not to be dictated to by the demands of their physical needs; it means that their minds are in charge of their bodies and not their bodies in charge of their minds. The self-awareness that cames from a change of lifestyle can be directed to Allah as an offering of the heart. That's why Muslims give up smoking, making love and other human pleasures during the daytime in Ramadan: it is an opportunity to discover your real self and rededicate yourself in the way you would like to, deep down.

Fasting takes place during Ramadan because that was the month that Muhammad received revelation through the angel Gabriel from Allah: it is obviously a very special time and it adds another dimension to the experience of fasting.

Some Muslim children start to fast a little when they are quite young, gradually building up, Ramadan by Ramadan, until the point that they can make a complete fast. Ideally, this is by the age of 10, but some are older than that when they can fast completely. This way their health is not damaged and they are not put off fasting altogether.

THE WHITE STREAK

At certain times of the year in certain parts of the world, dawn lasts for hours. It is helpful that the Qur'an gives Muslims the means to work out when "day" starts.

> Eat and drink until the white streak [of dawn] can be distinguished from the black thread [of night]. Then complete the fast until nightfall and have no dealings with women while you are secluded at your devotions in the mosques. Such are God's limits, so do not try to cross them. Thus God explains His signs to mankind that they may do their duty.
> (Qur'an 2: 187)

THE FAT AND THE LEAN

Fasting – or at least the ability to fast – has some unexpected benefits, and Sadi suggests that general lessons about life could be drawn from an experience like this!

> Once two young friends were travelling together. One who used to eat little became lean, while the other, who used to eat a lot, became fat. It so happened that they were taken prisoner on suspicion of spying. Each had his own cell in the prison.
>
> A week later, their innocence was proved and orders were issued to free them. When the doors of their cells were opened, people were astonished to find the lean man alive, and the fat man dead.

In some Muslim countries, there are signals to mark the beginning and ending of each day in Ramadan: in Bangladeshi villages a caller runs through the streets just before dawn breaks to warn Muslims that they must wake up to pray and eat before it is light; in Cairo a canon goes off at nightfall; and in Java flags mark that it is now the month of Shawal, which means it is no longer Ramadan. Congregational prayers will be followed by the social celebrations of Eid-ul-fitr.

When a wise man heard of their astonishment, he said, "Not this but the contrary would have been astonishing. The voracious eater could not resist hunger and perished, whilst the other could resist it and survived."

A sensible man practising moderation can face a calamity with courage. But the extremist, if forced by circumstances to practise moderation, finds hardships unbearable and perishes easily.

(Ashraf Abu Turab and Zia Sardar (eds.), A *Time to Speak: Anecdotes from Sadi Shiraz*, The Islamic Foundation, 1980, p. 25)

PROBLEM PAGE

Just before the month of Ramadan started a monthly journal for young Muslims featured a page of readers' questions and answers provided by experts. All the questions were about what to do or not do about fasting. The readers seemed sure that they *should* be fasting and they *wanted* to fast: they needed to know *how*. These are some of their questions:

Question:
There is a person who has not fasted for many years for various reasons but he does perform other duties such as prayer and Zakat. He then decides that he wishes to start fasting again, will he have to make up for the fasts he has missed or will he be punished for missing them?
Answer:
Missing the fast for any reason is a very big sin, if a Muslim misses any of the five pillars of Islam then he becomes close to Kufr. However, it is good if the person repents for his sinful act and starts to fast again. He will not have to observe all the fasts that he has missed as this would be unpractical because he has been missing them for so many years. He should do good deeds as often as possible and observe all the duties of a Muslim carefully. If he sincerely begs forgiveness from Allah then he will be forgiven.

Question:
If a person dies during the holy month of Ramadan before he has completed all the fasts can somebody else complete his fast for him?
Answer:
No, it is not permitted for somebody else to complete the fasts of a person who dies during Ramadan. This is because the remaining fasts of the dead person were no longer obligatory on him because the fasts are only compulsory for those who are present during the month of Ramadan. Allah does not ask us to do things that are beyond our capability. The remaining fasts of the dead person need not be made up by anybody.

Question:
If a woman has her monthly period during Ramadan, what should she do?
Answer:
During a woman's period it is not permitted for her to fast. The woman should not fast during her period but should make up for the missed fasts after Ramadan.

("Questions and Answers", *The Straight Path*, Vol. 7, No. 4, May 1986)

DYING AND MOURNING

When Muslims die their family or friends recite a line from the Qur'an which says that we all belong to Allah and will all return to him. Then they go to the home of the dead person to comfort the near and dear ones, to recite the Qur'an and to pray that Allah will forgive the one who has died.

Muslims of the same sex as the deceased wash the body and wrap it in a clean white cloth. They put it in a coffin or on a stretcher and men lift it onto their shoulders and carry it to the mosque or burial place.

At least some of the Muslims close to the person who died come together for *salat-ul-janazah*, funeral prayers. They make *niyyah* (intention) as they do at any prayer time, but on this occasion the *niyyah* is for the dead person. They stand in rows for prayer, facing the *qibla* (direction of Makka), with the coffin or stretcher in front of them. The mourners will also add *du'a* of their own.

THE LIVING AND THE DEAD

Dying can be compared to nightfall: it is a merging, and God is making it happen.

> You merge night into daylight,
> and daylight into night.
> You draw the living from the dead,
> and draw the dead from the living.
> You provide for anyone You will
> without any reckoning.
> (Qur'an 3: 27)

"The blood of the martyr is worth more than the ink of the scholar", *the Prophet said: action not words is what counts, even if that action leads to death. In some Muslim countries martyrdom is glorified, and dying for a cause is actively encouraged even though that death may be at the hands of Muslims fighting for other countries. Here in Iran the bodies are being buried of those who fell in the war with Iraq: they are treated as martyrs who gave their lives to defend Islam and their homeland. Perhaps at the same moment the funeral was taking place of Iraqi Muslims who were killed in the same battle...*

A MATTER OF HONOUR

It is very often at the point of death that the paradoxes of life become clear. This traditional story is a challenge to the view that life is "cheap".

A wandering Sufi, found in the desert, was brought to the tent of a wild Bedouin chief.

'You are a scout for our enemies, and as such we shall kill you,' said the chief.

'I am innocent,' said the Sufi.

'Do you see this sword?' asked the Sufi, drawing one; 'Before you can approach me I shall kill one of your men here. When I have done so, you will have a legitimate right to avenge his death. By so doing, I will save your honour, which is at this moment in grave danger of being sullied by shedding the blood of a harmless Sufi.'

(Idries Shah, "A Matter of Honour", *Caravan of Dreams*, Quartet Books, 1973, p. 145)

DON'T DELAY!

In Muslim countries, the dead are buried as soon as possible, partly for reasons of public health and partly to enable the mourners to release the full extent of their grief early on in their bereavement. When Muslims are in Britain they are sometimes distressed and frustrated by the delay in the permission to bury. Mrs Khan, a Pakistani woman living in England, speaks of her feelings on the matter:

When someone dies we are very sad, very sad.

As soon as the person dies we have to clean the mouth, close the eyes, and straighten the limbs of the body. Then a person comes to give the dead person a bath, and within eight hours we bury the person. In this country, though, it takes time: they don't release the body from the hospital, often for five or six days. And then, anyway, many people send the bodies to Pakistan — and I have told my husband and my children that if I die here, send me to Pakistan.

(Quoted in John Bowker, *Worlds of Faith*, Ariel Books, 1983, p. 247)

BELIEVING IN THE RESURRECTION OF THE DEAD

Death is natural, the end of a life in the body, Muslims say, but it is not the end and there is more life to come. *Akhirah* (life after death) is one of the three main Muslim beliefs: whereas our life now is temporary, *akhirah* is everlasting. It makes Muslims' present life meaningful, for they believe that all the good they do will be rewarded and all the bad punished. It is Allah who will decide this on the day of judgement – *Yawmul Akhirah* or *Yawmuddin*.

To appear in the court of justice, people have to be alive – that is, raised from the dead. Some non-Muslims don't believe in life after death or in eternal judgement, but Muslims reply that you cannot say definitely now that something won't exist and they should at least say that the afterlife is *possible*. They also point out that people will suffer terribly in the afterlife if they say they don't believe in it!

What is the problem? Muslims ask. Why couldn't Allah resurrect people? Didn't he create them?

AN ATOM'S WEIGHT

The final day is seen not simply as a spiritual experience but also as a physical and cosmic event.

When earth is shaken in her [final] quaking,
and earth throws forth her burdens,
and every man says: "What is wrong with her?"
On that day she will tell her news
since your Lord has inspired her to.
On that day men will appear in droves
to be shown their actions,
and whoever has done an atom's weight
of good will see it; while whoever
has done an atom's weight of evil
will see it.
(Qur'an 99: 1-8)

YOU'VE NO ONE BUT YOURSELF TO BLAME!

This *hadith*, recorded by a Sunni called An-Nawawi, is one that is called *qudsi*, meaning "holy" – that is, one in which the Prophet reported what had been revealed by Allah, though not necessarily in the actual words. This *hadith* began by speaking of Allah's forgiveness, which is there for the asking, and goes on to speak of God's power that humans can neither increase nor decrease.

O My servants, you will not attain harming Me

There are some things which never die: perhaps the love between a man and a woman who were so united in marriage that they could not imagine a life – even an afterlife – apart. This double grave in Turkey symbolizes their togetherness but also their distinctiveness: the wife is portrayed with a floral hat, the husband with a fez.

so as to harm Me, and you will not attain benefitting Me so as to benefit Me. O My servants, were the first of you and the last of you, the human of you and the jinn of you to be as pious as the most pious heart of any one man of you, that would not increase My kingdom in anything. O My servants, were the first of you and the last of you, the human of you and the jinn of you to be as wicked as the most wicked heart of any one man of you, that would not decrease My kingdom in anything. O My servants, were the first of you and the last of you, the human of you and the jinn of you to rise up in one place and make a request of Me, and were I to give everyone what he requested, that would not decrease what I have, any more than a needle decreases the sea if put into it.

O My servants, it is but your deeds that I reckon up for you and then recompense you for, so let him who finds good praise Allah and let him who finds other than that blame no one but himself.

(No. 24 in *An-Nawawi's Forty Hadith*, trs. Ezzeddin Ibrahim and Denys Johnson-Davies, The Holy Koran Publishing House, 1976, pp. 80-2)

THE POSSIBLE IMPOSSIBLE

Mrs Quereshi explains why it is so important to Muslims to bury the dead and not cremate them: it is not just a matter of personal preference or even a desire of the mourners to have a place to visit the dead, but a deep religious belief that we "need" our bodies for life after death. To many people the afterlife seems impossible, and that is why Mrs Quereshi says it is not the end of the world if cremation *does* take place. This whole aspect of our humanity is *about* making the impossible actually possible.

When a person dies, obviously his soul goes back to heaven. All that is left is the bones in the grave. Muslims believe — and I strongly believe in it — that on the Day of Judgement all the bones are put together and as a body we are going to answer for our deeds. So we believe you should not be cremated. But again, even if you've been cremated, it doesn't mean to say that God can't put you together. That is what a Muslim believes: he can make the impossible possible; so there's no problem.

(Quoted in John Bowker, *Worlds of Faith*, Ariel Books, 1983, p. 272)

DECLARING THAT MUHAMMAD IS THE PROPHET OF ALLAH

There have always been prophets in Islam: Adam, the first human, began the chain of prophecy that extends through many people that Christians and Jews have in their traditions, too, such as Moses and David. But Islam also has Hood, Enoch and other prophets that Jews and Christians don't recognize.

Belief in *risalah* (messages) is fundamental to Islam and these can come from people, angels or writing. The point is that Allah communicated with humanity and, from time to time, sent people to act as his messengers, bringing ideas, values and beliefs to others. Each *rasul* (prophet) carried part of the overall message. Muslims think the Prophet Muhammad, often called *rasullah, the* Prophet of Allah, was the "seal of the prophets". So Muhammad isn't the founder of Islam; he didn't begin Islam: he completed it.

There's always a danger that anyone who is highly praised could be idolized. In so many situations today, people who are famous for their ability or personality easily become pop heroes or cult figures. Religious leaders, especially founders of new movements, are even treated as if they were God themselves. The Muslim tradition has always been aware of this, and safeguards are built into Islam to prevent Muslims from praying to Muhammad or trying to communicate with his spirit in any way (even though great respect is shown to him, for example by saying "peace be upon him" after mentioning his name).

Muslims don't have paintings of Muhammad, say, in mosques or on the pages of the Qur'an, and there are no statues or models of the Prophet whatever. In a few parts of the Islamic world it has sometimes been fashionable to paint portraits of him, but even then the artists leave his face blank. Film producers have an interesting challenge as they make dramas and documentaries about the development of Islam. To create the impression that Muhammad is in a particular scene without actually depicting him they use the "voice over" technique and pose other characters "to camera" when they are having a conversation with Muhammad.

SENT BY GOD

As the Prophet of Allah, Muhammad had many different roles.

O Prophet, We have sent you as a witness, newsbearer and warner; and as someone who invites people to God by His permission, and as a shining lamp.
(Qur'an 33: 45-46)

LOVE ME, LOVE MY SUNNA

Tabaqat Ibn Sa'd recorded a tradition that the Prophet did not himself want to be idolized but did want everyone to treat the *sunna* – the Islamic way of life he was developing – in a grand way.

Hasan said that when Allah sent Muhammad, He said: "This is my Prophet, this is my chosen one; love him, and adopt his *sunna* and his path.
Doors are not locked up under him, nor do doorkeepers stand for him, and trays of food

are not served to him in the morning or the evening, but he sits on the ground and eats his food from the ground. He wears coarse clothes and rides on a donkey, with others sitting behind him, and he licks his fingers (after taking food). He says: "He who does not like my *sunna*, does not belong to me."

(Ahmad von Denffer, A *Day with the Prophet*, The Islamic Foundation, 1982, p. 3)

"Allah is the greatest. . .
I bear witness that there is no god but Allah. . .
I bear witness that Muhammad is Allah's messenger. . .
Rush to prayer. . .
Rush to success. . .
Allah is the greatest. . ."
When the simple masjid *in Madina was finished the Prophet chose Bilal, an African Muslim, to stand on the roof and call the* adhan, *as he had a strong, clear and pleasant voice. Nowadays, just before* salah, *five times a day, in mosques throughout the world, a man called a* muezzin *stands in the courtyard, or climbs a special tower called a* minar *(or minaret), and proclaims those traditional words Muhammad first taught to Bilal.*

MUHAMMAD BY NAME – MUHAMMAD BY NATURE?

In some Muslim societies it is not the thing to do to name a baby boy "Muhammad": no ordinary person should be associated with a human being so perfect as the Prophet. In other places boys have "Muhammad" as their first name but it is never actually used: they are called by their middle name; in that case they often just give the initial "M" when writing their name. There are some Muslim communities, however, where the boys are named *and* called "Muhammad", and the parents are thereby setting the boy an ideal to follow and in some sense giving him a special touch. A 14-year-old boy from Bangladesh, Muhammad Arfat Ullah, spoke about his name. His family call him "Arfat" but British friends – not knowing otherwise – call him "Muhammad". When asked if he minded, he said:

I am very pleased that I have "Muhammad" also for my name. It is altogether noble. But sometimes it is very difficult for me because he is *rasul* [prophet] and I am an ordinary boy!

DECLARING THAT THERE IS NO GOD BUT ALLAH

"Muhammad is the prophet of Allah" is the second part of the Shahadah (the declaration of faith which forms the first pillar of Islam). This belief is unique to Muslims; but the second part of the Shahadah – "There is no God but Allah" – is something that Christians, Jews and many other people can share with Muslims. It is an almost universal belief. So Muslims are, in fact, not playing with words but saying very simply that there is only one god. The belief in *tauhid* – the oneness and wholeness of Allah – is the very heart of Islam: everything else flows from it and into it. "Allah" is not one of God's names or even the Muslim name for God: Allah *is* God!

The opposites of *tauhid* are *kufr* (disbelief or atheism) and *shirk* (associating anything with Allah). The way humans normally relate and explain things cannot possibly apply to Allah. He was never born and will never die; he has no parents, no partners and no children. Allah is simply Allah! That is why there are no pictures of Allah – not because no one knows what Allah looks like but because Muslims say that Allah doesn't look like anyone or anything! He is a pure spirit who has no body: a body is limited by space but Allah is infinite; a body is limited by time but Allah is eternal. Therefore, to carve a model or draw a picture of Allah would be the opposite of worshipping him: Muslims say it would be idolatry.

Islamic art, even without figures, is far from boring. Many mosques, for example, are elaborately decorated and all of them are built to be attractive, inspiring places for Muslims to pray, study or meet in. The way this is done is ingenious and unique to Islam: it is done with three kinds of patterns.

Verses from the Qur'an are not only good to look at but should also help to instruct the believers, sometimes in a stimulating way, sometimes in a soothing way. The writing is often bold and colourful to catch Muslims' eyes and make them want to read it. Sometimes it is so fancy and stylized that it is impossible to make out even by Arabic readers! Occasionally, at a casual glance, you might not even realize that it was writing at all. The idea behind all this is that the Qur'an is a beautiful gift from Allah and the beauty can be seen in the form of the words as well as in their meaning.

The Arabs in the early Islamic days were extremely advanced mathematicians; they were interested in numbers and shapes and developed many theories about quantities and space. Their skill and their interest in mathematics can be seen in Muslim art, especially in the mosque. Lots of different shapes and patterns are used to explore the universe and to express subtly the belief that Allah has designed and constructed everything. When the shapes and patterns repeat themselves Allah is demonstrated as going on for ever.

A popular Muslim view of heaven is a garden of delight with shady groves and cool waters. This finds its way into Muslim art in the form of special swirling, flowery or leafy patterns (which are often called "arabesque" as they are thought to have originated in the Arab world). Arabesque is often blue, green or turquoise. It also repeats itself very often, showing that paradise, too, will last forever. Quite a lot of arabesque forms itself into rings or rectangles and other shapes which are empty in the middle. In this way, heaven is a secret, closed garden that is perfect by itself.

Quite often the three forms – the calligraphy (fancy writing), the geometry (shapes) and the arabesque are combined to make really rich complicated artwork using many different media and materials: drawing, painting, wood-carving, metal-chasing, glass-staining, ceramics, carpet-weaving, printing – all for the glory of Allah!

The will of Allah is also a motif in Muslim life: Muslims are often heard to say "Insh'Allah" (meaning "if Allah is willing") when hoping something will happen or trying to *make* it happen. Even so, people still have free choice and need to take decisions which will affect their lives and those of others, too. "Al qadr", the acceptance of destiny, means feeling that a new day will dawn tomorrow, that the situation is under control, that Allah is in charge and that, in the end, everything will be all right...

When you are sad or unwell not only do you need to get better but it can also help if you believe that somehow, deep down, everything's going to be all right. "Don't grieve. Really, Allah is with us," is the Muslim saying on this condolence card. In an ultimate experience such as mourning, many Muslims are drawn closer than ever to the ultimate being – to Allah.

THE OPENING

The Fatiha, which opens the Qur'an, has become the most frequently said Muslim prayer: it deals with first things first and captures the essential Muslim beliefs about Allah.

> *In the name of God, the Merciful, the Mercy-Giving*
> Praise be to God, Lord of the Universe,
> the Merciful, the Mercy-Giving!
> Ruler of the Day for Repayment!
> You do we worship and from You do we seek help.
> Guide us along the Straight Road,
> the Road of those whom You have favoured,
> with whom You are not angry,
> nor who are lost.
>
> [Amen]

(Qur'an 1: 1-7)

THE BLIND ONES AND THE ELEPHANT

This popular folk tale is thought to have originated with the mystic Rumi. Muslims are strong in their insistence that there is only one God, but that does prevent Sufis and other Muslims from saying that God appears in different ways to different people. Sharing ideas could lead to deeper understanding.

Beyond Ghor there was a city. All its inhabitants were blind. A king with his entourage arrived near by; he brought his army and camped in the desert. He had a mighty elephant, which he used in attack and to increase the people's awe.

The populace became anxious to see the elephant, and some sightless ones from among this blind community ran like fools to find it.

As they did not even know the form or shape of the elephant they groped sightlessly, gathering information by touching some part of it.

Each thought that he knew something, because he could feel a part.

When they returned to their fellow-citizens, eager groups clustered around them. Each of these was anxious, misguidedly, to learn the truth from those who were themselves astray.

They asked about the form, the shape of the elephant, and they listened to all that they were told.

The man whose hand had reached an ear was asked about the elephant's nature. He said: "It is a large, rough thing, wide and broad, like a rug."

And the one who had felt the trunk said: "I have the real facts about it. It is like a straight and hollow pipe, awful and destructive."

The one who had felt its feet and legs said: "It is mighty and firm, like a pillar."

Each had felt one part out of many. Each had perceived it wrongly. No mind knew all: knowledge is not the companion of the blind. All imagined something, something incorrect.

(Idries Shah, 'The Blind Ones and the Matter of the Elephant", *World Tales*, Allen Lane/Kestrel Books, p. 84)

THE SPIRIT IS WILLING

Writing to his son from prison where he faces possible execution, an Iraqi Muslim spoke about the benefits of religious faith.

Baghdad, 23rd Holy *Ramadhan*, 1380
March 10, 1961

Dear Abbas,

After presenting you my good greetings, I pray for your safety, success and guidance.

.... Herewith I am continuing my comments on your letter dated February 11, and my comments will continue through a few more letters, *insha' Allah*.

(1) The importance of religion for the individual.

The individual in this world, which is full of vicissitudes [changes], difficulties and disasters, feels a psychic security, and feels that he has a strong support and fortified refuge if he happens to be a believer with deep faith. He will feel that the universe has an Almighty who cares for him and includes him in his mercy and kindness, and who overwhelms him with his blessings and gifts,

and who exhilarates him with the greatness and beauty of his creation. The genuine believer realizes that the universe has an Almighty who is the source of goodness and blessings and who is the highest authority on truth, and justice, and the highest source for beauty and light. The believer is not a stranger in this universe, but a member of the family, and he came into existence in order to take part in the fulfilment of the great will and wisdom of Allah. The believer is happy, courageous, and forward-looking, irrespective of what is inflicted on him in terms of disasters or difficulties; contrary to the atheist who is overwhelmed with despair and despondency and who declares spiritual bankruptcy *vis-à-vis* [in the face of] catastrophes, for he knows of no value for life and no meaning for it outside his animal existence. That is why we observe these days a prevalence [a lot of] of nervous conditions among those whose religious spirit is weak, a condition which may lead to crime and suicide.

(Mohammad Fadhel Jamali, *Letters on Islam written by a Father in Prison to his Son*, World of Islam Festival Trust, 1978, p. 13)

DIFFICULT WORDS

akhirah belief in the resurrection of the dead and the day of judgement.

Allah Arabic name for "God".

hadith a tradition of the Prophet Muhammad; something that he himself said, not revealed by Allah; second in importance to the Qur'an.

higra (*hegira*) emigration of Muhammad and early Muslims from Makka and establishment of community in Madina in 622 CE – the beginning of the Islamic calendar.

ibadah worship of Allah; involves *iman* and *sadakah*.

iman faith, belief.

Jibreel (*Gabriel*) angel through whom Allah revealed his message to Muhammad for all humanity.

Ka'ba ancient cube-shaped monument in Makka, cleansed of idols by Muhammad; direction of prayer; central site of *hajj*.

khalifa (*caliph*) successor to Muhammad – four altogether; succession led to disputes and a division in the community.

kufr disbelief, atheism.

Madina originally called Yathrib; Muhammad and early Muslims settled there, and it became known as Madinat-ul-nabi, the city of the Prophet, shortened to Madina.

madrasah school or college for Islamic study, usually attached to a mosque.

Makka (*Mecca*) town in Saudi Arabia; birthplace of Prophet Muhammad; "capital" of Islamic world.

masjid (*mosque*) Islamic community centre and place of prayer and study.

Muhammad (*Mohammed*) "seal of the prophets", final messenger of Allah; received the Qur'an through angel Jibreel; honoured but not worshipped; named followed by the phrase "peace be upon him".

mulla title for leader in some Islamic societies.

niyyah sincerity, spiritual intention of prayer.

Qur'an (*Koran*) "recitation"; the compilation of all the revelations from Allah.

rasul messenger, prophet; *risalah* is an important Islamic belief in Allah's use of prophets and angels to communicate his message to humanity.

sadakah fairness, kindness – the basis of good relations between individuals and throughout society.

salah formal prayers offered five times a day by devout Muslims.

shariah Islamic law, divine in origin, covering all aspects of life.

shirk associating Allah with anyone or anything – that is, *not* believing Allah is whole and unique; polytheism.

sunna the Prophet Muhammad's way of life; in its significant aspects, *sunna* is followed by devout Muslims.

INDEX